"Alison and Matthew have done it again this time on one of the hottest but less understood technologies: blockchain. This is a book that any entrepreneur or business thinking about using blockchain to gain competitive advantage in their business should be reading."
Carlos Domingo, Co-Founder and CEO, Securitize

"Alison and Matthew were among the first to recognize the massive opportunities presented by blockchain technology. Their deep industry knowledge combined with decades of experience guiding strategy and investing in traditional markets should warrant the attention of anyone hoping to understand how to gain a competitive advantage in this new landscape."
Dan Elitzer, Founder, IDEO CoLab Ventures

"This book provides a great perspective from two blockchain insiders that truly understand both sides of the game—how to promote innovation and how to link it to traditional proven business models."
Alex Fedosseev, Founder, 1World Online

"Alison and Matthew are one of a kind. They both spent decades at the top of their fields yet still maintain the energy to venture to the frontier and help us all make sense of what's emerging."
Hunter Horsley, Co-Founder and CEO, Bitwise Asset Management

"Alison and Matthew have been on the forefront of investing in blockchain technology long before most people knew what it was. While many books provide theories and overviews, learn about investment strategies from two people who went beyond talking—to putting money to work shaping the technology's future."

Jalak Jobanputra, Founder and General Partner, Future\ Perfect Ventures

"Alison and Matthew have written a seminal book that helps the reader appreciate that we're on the precipice of massive block-chain-related wealth creation, and how to best position yourself for that coming blockchain revolution."

Lou Kerner, Co-Founder and General Partner, CryptoOracle

"Alison and Matthew's deep understanding of blockchain technology as well as vast knowledge in banking helped to inspire me to invent 'the multi-asset multi-blockchain gateway,' which allows seamless connectivity between Liquineq's blockchain or any other vendor's blockchain and blockchain firewall with deep smart contract inspection capabilities."

Dan Kikinis, Co-Founder Liquineq and Inventor with over 260 patents.

"In the fast-evolving world of decentralized networks, maintaining a competitive advantage becomes a dynamic challenge: Alison and Matthew have written a must-read book for entrepreneurs and investors alike that is aiming to stay on top of the opportunities it enables!"

Max Mersch, General Partner, Fabric Ventures

"Thirty years ago, we could talk to each other on the phone. And then the world started agreeing on a protocol for transferring information. Now we have GIFs, memes, blogs, Reddit, Twitter, and unlimited video calls. Today, we can send money via bank transfers. And we're seeing people starting to agree on protocols for transferring value. We can't even imagine the innovation around money and financial products to come."

Lasse Klassen, Founder, 1kx

"The scope of blockchain has not yet materialized. Think 'internet 1993.' Blockchain is as pertinent to the growth of the next ten years of cyberspace as the internet has been over the past 25 years."

Bill Sarris, Founder and CTO, Linqto

"There are a lot of great books on new technologies, and a few great ones on the blockchain. This one will join them and will be on my devices ready to be referred to because my life, and that of my firm, is dedicated to helping us all reach that better world towards which the innovators are working."

Bart Stephens, Co-Founder and Managing Partner, Blockchain Capital

BLOCKCHAIN
COMPETITIVE
ADVANTAGE

Also by Matthew C. Le Merle and Alison Davis

Blockchain Competitive Advantage

Build Your Fortune in the Fifth Era

Corporate Innovation in the Fifth Era

By Matthew Le Merle

Second Chance: A Novel

BLOCKCHAIN
COMPETITIVE
ADVANTAGE

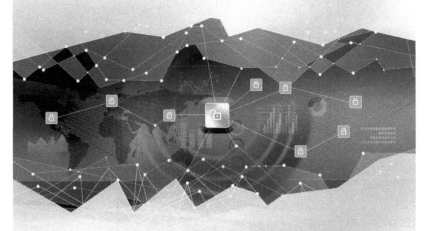

Whether you are an entrepreneur, investor, or established company,
learn how to win the battle for blockchain
competitive advantage.

ALISON DAVIS
MATTHEW C. LE MERLE

Fifth Era Media
4545 Paradise Drive,
Tiburon, CA 94920, USA
www.FifthEraMedia.com
415-994-4320

Originally published in the USA in 2019
By Fifth Era Media.

Fifth Era Media is a registered trademark of Fifth Era, LLC.

ISBN: 978-1-950248-04-9 (paperback)
ISBN: 978-1-950248-03-2 (hardbound)
ISBN: 978-1-950248-05-6 (ebook)

LCCN: 2019938150
Library of Congress Cataloging-in-Publication Data is available.

Editor: Nancy Pile
Designer: Robin Vuchnich

For all those who have pioneered in this new world—

this book reflects your insight and wisdom.

Visit

www.BlockchainCompetitiveAdvantage.com

to receive regular mailings and additional content about topics in
this book, and to find out more about the authors.

Contents

Abstract

Blockchain is moving into a new competitive phase that requires a clearer future view and more focused strategies for competing. Whether you are an entrepreneur, investor, or established company, learn how to win the battle for blockchain competitive advantage.

This book provides clear advice from two experts in strategy, technology investing, and blockchain. In its pages the authors:

- Establish a vision of the future and the big issues that need to be solved
- Describe the enabling innovations and technologies that may be leveraged
- Show you how to develop your strategy—making sure that you have a "way to play," that you understand the key success factors, and that you quickly secure a "right to win."

In blockchain a few of the leaders have begun to do just this, and they are preparing now for a much more competitive game—which is coming fast.

Foreword

Bart Stephens, Blockchain Capital

My journey into the fascinating world of blockchain technology and cryptocurrencies began in another world. A virtual world.

Prior to co-founding Blockchain Capital with my brother Brad in 2013, we spent 10 years as hedge fund managers investing in small cap technology stocks. One of our areas of investment expertise was investing in videogame companies. From 2002 to 2010, the videogame industry was going through a dramatic period of innovation in terms of new types of games and new business models. As life-long gamers ourselves, we natively understood the immersive power of virtual worlds, videogames, and digital assets. The categories of mobile gaming and social gaming were experiencing explosive growth on a global basis, especially in the US, China, and Korea. Traditional videogame companies were grappling with the shift in business model from packaged software to in-game item purchases and subscription-based business models like those of persistent world MMO (massively multiplayer online) games like World of Warcraft and Second Life.

Brad and I noticed that the large-scale MMO games had attractive recurring revenue models with users paying $15 per user per month for years at a time. Even more interesting was that many gamers were spending hundreds, thousands, even tens of thousands of dollars on in-game currencies. A funny thing happens when tens of millions of people inhabit a virtual world. They start acting like they do in the real world! They make social connections and virtual friends. They desire social recognition, wealth, and in-game status. These virtual worlds developed sophisticated in-game economies, and these economies had virtual currencies. Gamers started buying in-game currencies using real-world dollars to improve their game play, in-game wealth, and status.

In many ways, these in-game currencies were the precursors to cryptocurrencies, but they had significant limitations. Namely, they were owned by the videogame developer (not the gamers), and it was difficult to "cash out" into the real world of fiat, government-backed currencies.

We ended up investing in a company called IGE that created a digital asset exchange for in-game items and virtual currencies. IGE was looking at expanding into new markets and was evaluating acquisition opportunities. One of the acquisition targets was the infamous bitcoin exchange, Mt. Gox, that ultimately imploded. Brad was on the IGE board of directors, so we had a fiduciary responsibility to evaluate the acquisition target. We realized that meant doing research on bitcoin. IGE didn't end up buying Mt. Gox (phew!), but we decided to do a deep dive on the nascent blockchain sector. What followed was an intensive multi-month research process on bitcoin and blockchain technology. Down the bitcoin rabbit hole we went!

At the time, every single "serious" investor we knew was dismissing bitcoin out of hand, and many still are. To us, bitcoin didn't seem so strange as a result of our experience with videogame investing and in-game virtual currencies. We saw a global virtual currency in an open, censorship-proof network that could be exchanged for fiat currencies and could be used to purchase goods and services online. We started attending and eventually speaking at bitcoin meetups and conferences. We sought out academic researchers, cryptographers, bankers, engineers, lawyers, entrepreneurs, and fintech executives from my early career at E*TRADE.

As a result of our research project, we arrived at two conclusions. The first was that we believed that bitcoin was a super interesting, novel digital asset. It appeared to us like a venture-capital-type investment opportunity with a potentially enormous upside. This new asset had characteristics like a combination of Gold 2.0 and PayPal 2.0. It was an inflation-resistant, provably scarce digital asset that was inversely correlated to traditional assets like the stock market. It could also be used for payments on a global basis and had solved the "double spend" problem that had foiled earlier attempts at digital money. We started buying and mining bitcoin in early 2013. Our second conclusion was that the enabling technology of the blockchain could potentially be a game changer.

I like to say that the internet that we all use every day is really just the "internet of information"; it allows for the secure and instantaneous exchange of data. Blockchain technology is the "internet of value"; it allows for the secure and instantaneous exchange of value or assets.

Bitcoin was the proof of concept, but we saw a future where stocks, bonds, currencies, and commodities could potentially be traded and settled using blockchain technology. We wanted to invest in startups that would give us exposure to blockchain technology as a secular, multi-decade growth theme. To us, this was akin to investing in internet startups in the early 1990s.

We shared our views with early bitcoin investors in the sector like Barry Silbert of Second Market, Micky Malka of Ribbit Capital, Tim Draper of Draper Associates, and "Silicon Valley Bitcoin Patient Zero," Wences Casares of Xapo. We were mostly met with the response that bitcoin was all that mattered. While we loved bitcoin—and still do—to us it was the tallest tree in the forest, but we wanted to invest in the whole forest, not just one tree. We saw a future with multiple blockchain ecosystems.

When we couldn't find a VC fund to invest in that shared our worldview, we saw a market opportunity and co-founded Crypto Currency Partners, which would evolve to become Blockchain Capital. As we began investing in startups, we also wanted to draw upon the expertise of executives and investors with a more traditional financial services background. We were introduced to Alison Davis, and we were impressed by her and her financial services and corporate strategy experience and acumen. Alison became the chair of our advisory board and helped scale up our firm—the first venture capital firm focused entirely on blockchain technology.

Now in 2019, as I write this foreword to Alison and Matthew's book, blockchain is changing again. As a venture capitalist, I know that all new technologies go through a number of phases as they search for real-world acceptance. Early on, they are technologies looking for applications, and many never find them. For those that do, the early innovators struggle. They need insight and inspiration—that they often have. But they also need capital and backers that can bring them the relationships, capabilities, and assets—that most don't have.

Early-stage venture capitalists get involved, and that is exactly what we did in our funds backing great innovators like those at Bitwise, Coinbase, Circle, Kraken, and Ripple, as well as a host of others. Then, once the early proof of concepts have taken root, and users, revenue, and cash flow begin to flow to the early and most successful projects and startups, the world begins to climb on-board. More capital arrives, brought by established investors who now want to participate. Established companies that had initially poured cold water and scorn over the innovators now proudly launch their own initiatives. Governments begin to compete for the hearts and minds of the innovators. Before we know it, there are a host of competitors going after every end point and use case.

That is where we are right now. Blockchain has arrived in its early competitive phase, and firms like Blockchain Capital—and our partnership team of Brad, Spencer Bogart, and me—know that it is no longer enough to provide capital and a great deal of support and added value. Now we need to find ways to make sure that the teams we back get a long way ahead of the pack—that they capture competitive advantage.

This book unpacks this specific question: how do we gain competitive advantage in the coming phase of intense competitive activity that we see on the horizon of blockchain protocols, in which we have invested so much of our personal time and effort? There is a battle beginning that will change our world for the better. However, every entrepreneur, investor, and established company should think long and hard about how they plan to make their blockchain projects successful ones. This book, written by two people whom we know very well and immensely respect, can help them do so.

There are a lot of great books on new technologies and a few great ones on the blockchain that I have on my real-world nightstand or on my digital bookshelf. This one will join them and will be on my devices ready to be referred to because my life, and that of my firm, is dedicated to helping us all reach that better world towards which the innovators are working.

Let's make this a reality together.

Bart Stephens
Co-Founder and Managing Partner
Blockchain Capital
San Francisco, California, USA

Preface

For over 15 years we were strategy advisors to companies like Bank of America, Blackrock, Chase, eBay, Google, HP, Microsoft, Pay-Pal, Visa, and others. We worked as consultants, senior partners, and practice leaders at the strategy firms McKinsey, AT Kearney, Booz, and Monitor, and helped clients create corporate strategy, go-to-market plans, partnerships and acquisitions, launch new products, and build new innovation capabilities.

The last two decades we have been focused on investing in technology and financial services companies, and serving as board directors of companies in these sectors. Alison was the CFO of Barclays Global Investors, which is now Blackrock—the world's largest institutional investment management firm—and then as managing partner of Belvedere Capital—a regulated private equity firm focused on acquiring banks and financial services companies. She has served as a board director of First Data Corporation, Fiserv, Royal Bank of Scotland, City National Bank, Unisys, Xoom, Presidio Bank, and many others. Matthew did a stint as head of strategy and marketing for Gap Inc., just as its brands were launching their online and digital presence, and now is a general partner of Keiretsu Capital, which provides access to the best early-stage technology startups through a series of funds and helps lead the world's most active early-stage investment network.

Together we are GPs of a blockchain fund of funds that we have created with Keiretsu Capital where we back the best blockchain venture capital firms. One or the other of us is also an advisor at Blockchain Capital, BitBull Capital, Bitwise, Codex, Hadron, London Block Exchange, Linqto, Liquineq, ReadyUp, Securitize, Spark, and others. Our own family office, Fifth Era, backs teams that understand digital commerce, content, and fintech technologies, including blockchain.

Early in 2019 we had just finished reading a large number of 2019 "outlook for blockchain and crypto" articles posted online and in traditional publications. They were interesting and thought provoking, but inevitably, because the authors focused on a one-year outlook, they ended up being very tactical. What upgrades and new features should we expect from the leading blockchain protocols? What price do we predict for bitcoin or other leading cryptocurrencies? Which blockchain development platforms will gain strength this year?

Furthermore, most of the time the postings were also highly technical. That is obviously relevant for the developer community in this timeframe, but it also means the reader can "miss the forest for the trees" because the very platform upon which you are building may not be around in the future. Why? Because you may be one of a plethora of projects competing for the same opportunity and others may capture the key points of advantage first; or because some other development protocol will become the better place to base your decentralized application (DAPP) given the market it is focused on. And so on.

How do you ensure you do not "miss the forest for the trees"?

How do you establish a longer-term view to make sure you are not blindsided by being overly focused on the short term?

Given our experience helping large corporations as well as fast-growth early-stage companies answer this question, we found ourselves then discussing what happens when you cross the fundamentals of competitive strategy with this new, emerging world of blockchain and crypto. This discussion led us to sit down and write this book.

The title of this book also speaks to our view of the long-term importance of blockchain to society. We believe the blockchain protocol represents an opportunity to take a great leap forward into an even more powerful digital world. One in which old-fashioned notions of how to ensure identity, trust, security, and so on, are replaced by powerful, ubiquitous new ways of accomplishing our desired ends. The digital infrastructure we have today will not be sufficient for the future. We need to evolve to a digital world that incorporates native digital monies and assets, and blockchain provides the promise that it may give birth to those important innovations.

It is our observation that more than 10 years after the publication of Satoshi Nakamoto's seminal paper "Bitcoin: A Peer-to-Peer Electronic Cash System," we are finally entering a competitive phase of blockchain's development. We wanted a title that captured this new phase and the focus it will engender. Hence, the inclusion of the words "competitive advantage"—because this is always the focus of good strategy in highly competitive markets and industries.

We hope you enjoy reading this book and that you will get

some ideas that will help you win, regardless of whether you are a blockchain entrepreneur, an investor, or an established company entering the fray.

Alison Davis
Matthew C. Le Merle
San Francisco, California, USA

Executive Summary

After almost 200 years living in the Industrial Era, humankind is now entering a new era driven by the twin forces of the digital and life sciences revolutions. Today we are all connected, and nearly all the world's information is online. Every industry has been impacted, and many have gone through fundamental transformations. We have also begun not only to edit and adjust our plants and animals, but are on the edge of the societal discussion as to whether to alter the very nature of human beings (in this book we do not focus on the future impact of life sciences innovations).

It is a time of great opportunity, and also great uncertainty and even fear. It is a time of unprecedented disruption and creative destruction, and also a time of enormous value and wealth destruction and creation. The greatest that the world has ever seen. We call this the Fifth Era, and in our previous books—*Build your fortune in the fifth era* and *Corporate innovation in the fifth era*—we have written about how individuals and corporations can prepare to be successful rather than left behind in this new era.

In these books we detail the essential changes underway. We make the point that this is not just about one or two major technological shifts. Rather, we are living in a time of unprecedented change in which a breadth of compounding innovations—the like of which we have never seen before—the internet, artificial intelligence, the internet of things and the sensor revolution, 3D manufacturing and the distributed maker movement, augmented reality, clean energy technologies, gene editing, quantum computing, blockchain, and many others—are all coming together in the same timeframe to propel us into a completely new era of human life on planet Earth. We call this the "Fifth Era."

Among these innovations are several that will be important in the context of the narrative of this book:

- The internet—invented in the 1970s and ramped up over the last 20 years—has already had a huge impact on human life—how we work, communicate, do commerce, socialize, learn, etc. However, it is creaking under the weight of several serious issues. It was invented as a communication platform for scientists to share data and so was not designed to cope with the implications of being turned into a commerce platform. These are the five big issues that need resolution:
  - Security
  - Identify and Trust
  - Concentration and Control
  - Lack of Native Digital Payments
  - Lack of Native Digital Assets
- The blockchain protocol that was invented to support the first global electronic money without a state sponsor. We will make the case that this new technology has the potential to solve the five big issues that the communications

internet needs to resolve. Billions of dollars of capital and many of the brightest technical minds of our time are flooding into the space to see how to apply the protocol to make a fully digital world a possibility.

- Meanwhile, with the blockchain protocol came other innovations—foremost among them is the creation of cryptoassets and tokenization as well as the funding innovation of initial coin offerings (ICOs). These also hold great promise for assisting us in moving towards our digital future.

However, it is very early in both the development of these new technologies and the business innovations that they can and will drive. Lots will change, every industry will be impacted, but in the process many projects and players will fail. Entrepreneurs will work hard only to find they can't get traction before their resources run out. Investors will lose money more often than they see a return even if the overall return is an attractive one. Established companies will have varying degrees of success in adapting and retaining their positions. Trillions of dollars of value will be lost and gained. Just as it was 20 years ago when we first rolled out the internet and connected the world. Several of the world's largest companies today by market capitalization didn't exist 25 years ago, and others that were much admired are not relevant any longer.

This time around, we want to be smarter and use the learnings of the past to inform decision-making and the allocation of time and capital.

For those of us who have spent a large part of our lives in Silicon Valley and in early-stage technology investing, we can see that this new wave of innovation and change is beginning to show the same hallmarks of similar waves of the past. As the current innovation wave moves into a more competitive phase, well-capitalized projects and companies begin to jockey for traction and position. Additionally, challenges come to light in regard to moving from prototype and proof of concept, to global rollouts of new value propositions. What we notice is that the current innovation issues are moving to the same beat that we have seen in the past with other global software transformations. This includes, most importantly of all, the global rollout of the internet.

This time many of the players are first-time entrepreneurs; new investors entering early-stage technology investing for the first time; or established companies new to embracing new technologies and innovation agendas looking to reinvent their businesses to be "fit for future." However, this does not mean that everyone needs to go back to first principles and figure it all out from scratch. It seems to us it makes more sense to capture the learnings of the past—the best practices of competitive strategy, entrepreneurialism, investing, and corporate innovation—and see which apply to this new blockchain-inspired wave of change.

At the same time, we don't believe you can simply take traditional strategy approaches that were created for competing in established industries and apply them to this world of innovation and rapid change. Indeed, we believe that when seeking competitive advantage in emerging spaces and when creating "new-to-the-world" products and services meeting needs most customers don't even know that they have, a new strategy framework is required.

UCLA professor Richard Rumelt recounts Steve Jobs' answer

to the question, "What is your long-term strategy?" Jobs' respond-
ed, "I am going to wait for the next big thing." We believe we are
on the brink of a "next big thing"—with the shift of our communications internet to its future state as a commercial internet.

So we have written this book, building on our experience
working with entrepreneurs scaling up to be among the winners;
working with investors trying to identify those businesses that
have a higher chance of success; and working with established
companies pursuing innovation strategies to ensure their business
is "fit for future" success.

To work through this complex topic on behalf of three different constituencies—entrepreneurs, investors, and established
companies—the book is structured as follows:

- We begin with an introduction to innovation-based strategy or competitive advantage and some important core
  concepts that will flow through the rest of the book.
- In Part I, we provide a vision of the future with regard
  to the continuing migration towards a fully digital world.
  This future view is important for the formulation of
  strategy since it is with this perspective that you can begin
  to make choices about what to focus on and what value
  propositions to make happen in its context. A view to the
  future entails having a keen appreciation of the big issues
  that end users and society at large want to see resolved.
  Resolution of these issues is crucial because it forms the
  raw material from which powerful business visions and
  value propositions are built where disruptive innovations

are concerned. This also is the focus of Part I.

- In Part II, we take a closer look at the new innovations and technologies that new players can leverage to build their competitive strategy. We first look at the invention of bitcoin and show how it has the potential to address the internet's critical shortcomings. We then review each of these—the blockchain protocol, cryptoassets and tokenization, and initial coin offerings—and provide a perspective on how these innovations can be helpful.

- In Part III, we move to the specific issue of competitive advantage for each of entrepreneurs, investors, and established companies, with some initial thoughts for governments too. In this part of the book, we focus on competitive strategy as it relates to picking a "way to play" and being clear about the key success factors that will turn this into a "right to win." We also detail tactics and best practices that have worked in the past and which we believe will be helpful in the context of the blockchain opportunity too.

Together these parts—I, II, and III—lay out an approach we have seen reap success for those seeking competitive advantage in spaces characterized by rapid innovation and change. This approach has been informed by our work with leading disruptive players like eBay, Google, Microsoft, and PayPal, and dozens of disruptive early-stage companies that have staked out a business in a new and emerging field.

We hope you find it helpful.

Introduction
Innovation-Based Competitive Advantage

Competitive strategy aims to establish a profitable and sustainable position against the forces that determine industry competition.

—*Michael Porter*

Prediction is very difficult, especially if it's about the future.

—*Niels Bohr*

When we set competitive strategy for established companies, we don't begin with the one-year outlook. We always start further out and then work backwards. We are looking to determine long-term competitive advantage in markets and industries where multiple well-capitalized competitors are going head-to-head to win.

In some industries with long lead times and capital cycles, we start 10 and more years into the future. In rapidly changing industries, sometimes we start three or five years out—because the pace of change may invalidate longer-term views before we get to them. We don't try and make point predictions. Instead, we look for possible future outcomes or scenarios. We look for key issues that need to be resolved and key success factors (KSFs), actions that are likely to enhance the chance of winning by blocking out competitors or making them fail. Then we use those insights to inform the short-term action plan—the traditional annual plan.

What happens when you cross the fundamentals of traditional competitive strategy with the new, emerging world of blockchain and cryptoassets? This is the fundamental question we try to answer in this book.

Traditional Corporate Strategy Approaches Are Insufficient

Much as we admire the body of work that theorists have developed for setting strategy in established markets, we find, more often than not, it is insufficient for new industries and disrupted markets—in which the very nature of user demands are either emerging or still to be surfaced; where the most promising products and services of the future have not yet become apparent; and where the basis of competition has not yet been established.

Steve Jobs, who was on the board of directors at Gap during Matthew's tenure there, was vocal in his view that innovators create their own demand by imagining "new-to-the-world" products that meet needs the end user did not even know they had. The innovator imagines their industry into existence and delights users with their inventions—rather than analyzing the user and their current behaviors in order to figure out how to get started. Once that future is imagined, only then do you work backwards to figure out what needs to be done to get there.

Most corporate strategy approaches begin with the assumption that needs have already been defined and that products and services are already in the marketplace. Accordingly, it follows that it is quite possible to determine the value of better cost, quality, or service. Analysis is conducted to segment users into groups, to define what they value most, and to assess the best ways to deliver that value along the value chain. This provides a rich understanding for determining where you are best equipped to play, the things you will focus on doing relative to your competitors to win, and if you can deliver, to eventually capture a competitive advantage over them.

How does all of this play out in the Fifth Era—an era where new-to-the-world technologies and innovations are surfacing new needs, allowing for completely new business models and redefining industries so that the very definition of an industry and a competitive set is changing before our eyes? How does this apply to the next evolution of the internet and the competition that is coming between those who are addressing the issues that are currently challenging its effectiveness—for example, security and identity and trust? How does this apply to the blockchain protocol and those who seek to apply it?

What Is the Objective Function?

Before we get started, we have to ask the question—what are we trying to maximize? What is our objective function?

In traditional frameworks the answer is economic value. Whether you are an entrepreneur, investor, or established company, your objective can be boiled down to a common one of capturing as much economic value as possible—the discounted value of future cash flows or profit streams. This has driven capitalist economies since the arrival of the Industrial Era and is widely viewed as the driving force in business and investing today.

It is possible to argue with this perspective, and leading theorists and figures are beginning to do so. At the sovereign level governments as far apart as Beijing and Brussels are beginning to explore setting the objective function to explicitly incorporate other non-monetary considerations. Governments are beginning to look at measures such as citizen happiness or well-being indices. Investors, such as Blackrock, State Street, Schroeders, and many others, are beginning to ask companies these two questions: what useful important purpose do you serve to society? Are you are able to create sustainable value or profit that doesn't create external costs on society—like stressful jobs, toxic products, large carbon footprints, or damage to local communities?

Many of today's successful corporate leaders are taking a broader view of their role than just the creation of short-term/near-term profit. And boards of directors are beginning to discuss how their governance role must expand to include overseeing a healthy corporate culture and ensuring the company is a good corporate citizen; or at a minimum, ensuring the company avoids being a bad one that inflicts harm on certain stakeholders in the pursuit of profit.

In the blockchain community this rejection of a simple economic-value-maximizing objective is also widespread—indeed, many reject it completely.

For this book, we believe successful entrepreneurs and companies in the Fifth Era will more than ever need to have a strategy that can build sustainable competitive advantage—that creates real customer value and is able to gain market share and profits against tough competitors.

However, we believe in order to attract capital and talent as well as increasingly conscious millennial customers, they will also need to have a meaningful purpose—describing how they are making the world a better place, not worse. And they will need to avoid knowingly or carelessly "doing harm"—hurting employees (e.g., stressful or dangerous jobs, hostile employee environments, etc.), damaging the environment (e.g., pollution, mountain-top removal, heavy carbon footprints, etc.); or selling products and service that have negative external impacts.

Boards of directors and CEOs have seen how quickly reputation, stock price, and regulatory standing can be damaged from missteps in these areas—and it is becoming much harder to hide bad behavior or accidental negligence in our current digital world. In this book, we focus mostly on what is required to build sustainable competitive advantage in an economic sense. But we fully support the notion that these other elements will be increasingly important, and we encourage our readers to take a broader view of building a successful company.

An Approach for Establishing Innovation-Based Strategy

Over the years of working with dozens of disruptive technology companies, including players like eBay, Google, Microsoft, and PayPal, seeking competitive advantage in spaces characterized by rapid change and disruptive innovation, we have found it is important to avoid overly complex frameworks and approaches. We have found it best to do the following:

- Begin with a vision of the future and the big issues that need to be solved in that future.
- Understand the enabling innovations and technologies that may be leveraged.
- Develop your strategy—make sure you have a "way to play," you understand the key success factors (KSFs), and you can quickly secure a "right to win."

Let's briefly talk about each in turn.

Begin with a Vision of the Future and the Big Issues to Be Addressed

Beginning with Steve Jobs' proposition that the end users can't help us because they don't know how to talk about something they have never seen, we need to create our own vision of what we believe the future will look like. That doesn't mean that we don't speak to end users, watch what they do, and imagine how it might be made better. But that is input rather than the source of insights that we are seeking and around which we will build our strategies and competitive advantages.

This is the focus of Part I of this book. In it we describe one vision for the future—we describe a fully digitally-enabled world that has completed the transition from an internet based on communication to one that is designed to fully enable commerce. This is not the only vision of the future—we don't try and explore the future of healthcare, of environmental change, or of a number of other aspects of the future that may be about to change in profound ways. However, we think having a strongly developed sense of where our digital economy is heading is itself likely to be a major advantage for many industries and businesses.

Doing this future vision work is one of the topics we discuss elsewhere, so we won't belabor the topic here. However, Sidebar 1 describes a few of the tools that can be useful. Armed with this vision we then explore what issues need to be resolved in order for the world to migrate to the future vision. In Part I, we also lay out five specific issues that we see as needing to be resolved for the future vision we are describing.

Sidebar 1: Tools for Developing Innovation Strategies

There are a number of methodologies that can be very helpful to leadership teams in surfacing potential areas of innovation that can either be used to create a competitive advantage or that need to be defended against. These methodologies are designed to help leaders manage in a future of uncertainty and are created to loosen and/or broaden the mindset of the leadership team, preparing them to consider alternative directions and identify needed areas of innovation and change.

While we will not fully describe these methodologies in this book, they include scenario planning, dynamic ecosystem management, industry-level wargaming, and disruptor analysis. Our former partners, Peter Schwartz (1996, 2000), Eamonn Kelly (2005), and Peter Leyden (2000), have all written extensively on scenario planning and its use to help corporate leaders think more broadly about the future and about innovation in strategy and decision-making.

In 2005, we worked with Eamonn conducting scenario-planning exercises to help our client HP, one of the most innovative technology companies of the Industrial Era, come to terms with the rapidly changing world and its need for new forms of information technology products and services. Having explored future uncertainties and plausible scenarios, we were able to facilitate a large group of HP executives in defining the most likely future technology domains for HP, including blade computing, the cloud, distributed computing, mobility, cybersecurity, and so on. Kevin Kelly of *Wired* magazine was an external expert in that scenario-planning program and did a great job helping shift the mindset of our client by changing the framing of the discussion.

Meanwhile, our former colleague at AT Kearney, Paul Laudicina (2012), helped shape many executives' mindsets through his work on scenario planning and on building strategies for the future. As chairman emeritus of the consulting firm AT Kearney and current chairman of the Global Business Policy Council, Paul shares our view that it is critical for business leaders to think about the future in times of change and uncertainty, and to evaluate the robustness of their strategies in different future environments.

Ecosystem mapping, industry-level wargaming, and disruptor analysis serve as powerful tools for mapping likely directions of future industry development and directions from which new disruptive innovations and competitors may surface. At PayPal and StubHub we used these tools to map out these issues, surface priorities for the innovation strategy, and sequence which new innovations each respective company should bring to market.

Disciplined methodologies for building strategies in times of uncertainty are, however, few in number. Most large companies are very adept at defining plans for the businesses they already have, in conditions they are already experiencing. In this time of change, it is much more difficult to decide where to focus with regard to new technologies and opportunities that may be surfacing and disrupting existing operations and competitive positions. Greater rewards will accrue to those who are able to plan ahead and be more clear-eyed about possible futures.

Source: Le Merle, M., & Davis, A. (2017). *Corporate innovation in the fifth era.* Cartwright Publishing.

Understand the Enabling Innovations and Technologies

Armed with a keen appreciation of how the world will shift and what big issues will have to be resolved, it is at this point, and not before, that powerful new technologies and innovations become relevant. It is dangerous to begin with a technology and go out looking for applications. More often than not, failure lies that way. Instead, you first establish the future vision and begin to think through the big issues that need solving. After that, you then take a look at the world's emerging technologies and business innovations to see which of them you can leverage into your plan to create a source of competitive advantage.

In this book, our focus is on blockchain and the innovations that have been built around it—the blockchain protocol itself, cryptoassets and tokenization, and the way in which technology has been used to enable fundraising through initial coin offerings

(ICOs). This does not mean that these are the only enabling technologies that may be valuable. As mentioned above, we believe that there are a host of other technologies, such as artificial intelligence, the sensor revolution, and augmented reality, to name but three, which may also be leverageable. In Part II of this book, we take a deeper look at the blockchain-related innovations and how they may apply to capturing competitive advantage.

Develop Your Strategy

In order to develop a strategy with a high likelihood of creating competitive advantage, it is necessary to move through three phases: first, make sure you have a coherent "way to play"; second, understand the key success factors (KSFs) for that "way to play"; and finally, ensure that you can quickly secure a "right to win" by capturing the KSFs. Each is discussed in turn.

Make Sure You Have a Way to Play

Now that you have defined the future vision and the big issues that need to be resolved, and have an appreciation for some of the innovations and technologies that may be leverageable, you can then look hard at where you are beginning and see if you have a "way to play"—if you have the basis for beginning on the long journey towards competition and success.

In really fast-moving areas of disruptive innovation often very few people have an inbuilt way to play. This can be an opportunity. Often we have found that startups can begin to play even though they appear to have very little in the way of capabilities and assets at the outset. However, what they do have is very powerful: a clear vision, a grasp of what issues to focus on, deep understanding of the latest innovations and technologies, and a motivated founding team. This is often enough to move to the next step. In Part III, we begin to explore this issue, with strategies that entrepreneurs, investors, and established companies are exploring with regard to blockchain.

Understand the Key Success Factors (KSFs)

Now you identify the handful of things that really matter—the key success factors (KSFs) that will be critical to turn your way to play into a "right to win."

In the future that you have painted and given the way you plan to play, what really matters? Can you condense it down to just a handful of the most important topics?

Usually you are looking for a finite number of capabilities that, were you to have them and if you were the best at them, might make you the winner. This is not a generic step. It is very dependent upon your chosen way to play. As a result, no book can do a good job at detailing every KSF for every business strategy—indeed that would not be possible. However, in Part III, we begin to surface some of those KSFs for each of entrepreneurs, investors, and established companies.

Quickly Secure a Right to Win

Once it all starts, everything becomes chaotic and confusing. There are so many things to think about, so many conflicting claims on time and resources, so few of anything compared to what is needed for the task at hand.

The best entrepreneurs and corporate innovators we have worked with don't let the chaos get them down. They stick resolutely to the task at hand, which is to simply focus on the KSFs and find any and every way to secure them; to get them locked down; to steal them away before the next player can get them. This is how they shift their way to play into capturing a right to win.

Focus is important—a single-minded determination to get those KSFs before anyone else can. Intense execution every day, but against that long-term vision and future that you painted at the outset. This is the focus of Part III of the book, where we indicate the sorts of considerations that go into achieving a right to win, whether you are an entrepreneur, investor, or established company. We also have a few thoughts in this part of the book for governments too.

Then the focus shifts to being flexible and ready to adjust as needed since you almost certainly did not get the future vision, big issues, or KSFs right at the beginning of the journey. But who could have? The need to pivot is almost a cliché in innovation hubs and networks.

So, with that as context, in the next chapters we will begin exploring the exciting opportunity ahead of us. We are in the beginning stages of the next evolution of our digital economy, and blockchain technologies will give rise to incredible value-creation opportunities. There are already many pioneers hard at work in the space. But as in prior eras, many will fail, and the winners—entrepreneurs, investors, established companies—will be those that can determine how to create sustainable competitive advantage.

Part I | Unfinished Digital Revolution

Chapter 1
Our Communications Internet

The Web as I envisaged it—we have not seen it yet. The future is still so much bigger than the past.

—Tim Berners-Lee

As noted in the previous chapter, Steve Jobs' answer to the question, "What is your long-term strategy?" was "I am going to wait for the next big thing." That time has come with the shift of our communications internet to its future state as a commercial internet and the realization of a truly digital world. In this chapter, we begin by explaining why the internet we have is not the one that we will end up with—indeed, it is fundamentally challenged in many ways—as we make the shift to a future vision of a completely digitalized world.

Why Do We Do the Things We Do?

When the arrival of the internet ushered in the digital world that we all live in today, it was easy to miss the direction and speed with which our world would change. We grew up in a physical world, so when people began to say that we would give up the patterns, behaviors, and beliefs of our youth, we could not really envision what that might mean. We had very little idea of what the near future would hold and couldn't have imagined we would be, for example, using email, texts, and instant messages instead of sending letters and leaving voicemails on answering machines; using online websites and later our mobile phones to manage our money rather than writing and receiving checks and visiting our local bank; ordering books, groceries, and many other things from a small round device that listens, places our order, and magically gets everything delivered the next day for free rather than taking hours to visit physical stores and choosing from the merchandise on display.

It took some imagination to envision how the early internet would change our lives, and we failed more than we succeeded in scoping the future. We were not alone. Most of the world's largest and most sophisticated companies had great difficulty decoupling from their pasts and fully envisioning this digital future. Many watched as their core businesses were first nibbled at and then gulped down by voracious new competitors.

Alibaba, Alphabet/Google, Amazon, Apple, Facebook, Microsoft, and Tencent, plus a host of others, rose to prominence as they fully leveraged the new internet with its protocols of TCP/IP, FTP, frame relay, and others. And so they built enormous new businesses on top of computer science breakthroughs that leapt from the lab and addressed needs users did not even know they had.

As George Orwell put it so succinctly, "To see what is in front of one's nose needs a constant struggle."

Of course it does not make sense to send pieces of paper around the world—when we can communicate in real-time electronically. Of course it does not make sense to search for information printed on paper, bound into books, stored on shelves in libraries—when the world's information can be digitized and made available to everyone, everywhere, at any time. Of course it does not make sense to ship products to small brick boxes on every corner and hope that someone comes in and finds what they want from the tiny stock that physical space can hold—when instead the world's bounty in every shape and size can be held centrally and released on demand to whoever needs that particular SKU; or made to order.

Yes, indeed, but much easier to see in hindsight. Because just as obviously, it makes no sense that we keep gold under our mattresses as the medieval squires once did. It makes no sense that we jealously guard our private ledgers in which we jot down our business dealings with others—keeping each transaction secret, so only we know who to trust and who to avoid. It makes no sense that we suffer filling out little sheets of paper in quadruple to be filled out in each step of every shipping process that brings everything we need and want to our homes and businesses—slowed and made costly and bureaucratic because the clerks still work the way the Medici did 500 years ago. It makes no sense that we continue to transact our commercial and financial dealings through banks, credit agencies, payments companies, and a plethora of other players who created our financial system during the Industrial Era but who have not yet figured out how to migrate it to be native within the internet that we use today.

We can't see what is in front of us and just how irrational it all is. Surely if we could, we would have changed these things—if we knew how.

Now a new protocol has arrived—the blockchain protocol. Once again, our most fundamental understanding of how things work is being turned upside down. Many of us are struggling to understand the brilliance of a protocol that enables us to break from past ways of doing things that make no sense at all once you look closely; ways of doing things which are slow and costly, and don't really meet our needs.

Before we can turn to blockchain, we need to first look at the internet we have. We will see that we are only partway to completing our digital revolution. We have built the communications protocols but lack the commerce protocols.

The Early Years

The internet we have, which has been so powerful in changing every industry and every aspect of human endeavor, was intended to be a computer communications platform. It was never intended to be a commerce platform.

In 1973, when David Boggs and Robert Metcalfe first invented Ethernet, they did it for a very narrow reason—to help computers communicate with each other over short distances. Metcalfe had been working on hardware at MIT for the Advanced Research Projects Agency Network (ARPANET) and had based his dissertation on the connecting together of computers into networks. The two met when they were working at Xerox Palo Alto Research Center (PARC). They were intrigued by the experiments being conducted as part of the ALOHAnet, created at the University of Hawaii, which had demonstrated the first public example of a wireless packet data network in 1971. While full of bugs, the ALOHAnet demonstration made it possible for two computers to "speak" to each other. Ethernet took things a step further and in a more reliable way. Before long many computer scientists were building on this foundation to find even more powerful ways for computers to communicate with each other.

By 1976, Vint Cerf and Bob Kahn, working together, invented the TCP/IP protocols (transmission control protocol and internet protocol) that are at the heart of the internet as we know it. Bob Kahn had been working with ARPANET and, as early as 1972, had been able to link up to 20 computers together. By 1973, he had moved on to the Defense Advanced Research Projects Agency (DARPA). It was here that he got the inspiration for what became the TCP protocol while working on a satellite network project. The concept was to have an open-architecture that would allow any computer to freely speak with any other despite differences in hardware or software used on their specific platforms. When Cerf joined Kahn at DARPA, together they solidified the protocols.

Importantly, in the 1970s, no one could have predicted the uses to which these experimental protocols would eventually be put, and so issues, such as the global security risks of public networks, were not anticipated. Neither TCP nor IP were intended to be "cyber secure" protocols, which led to vulnerabilities from the outset. Similarly, TCP/IP were created for wired networks, and some of the fundamental issues of congestion that we experience today can be traced back to this wired birth.

In parallel with the breakthroughs in network protocols, researchers at the Stanford Research Institute (SRI) were working on the issue of how to simplify and standardize the addressing of computers connected together by a network. Their innovation was to create a text file named HOSTS.TXT that mapped names to numerical addresses of computers on the ARPANET. Over at ARPANET the directory, maintained by Elizabeth Feinler, eventually became the WHOIS directory. It gave rise to the concept of domain name addresses where different types of locations would receive different suffixes (for example, educational addresses would receive the suffix ".edu"). Meanwhile, the maintenance of numerical addresses, called the Internet Assigned Numbers Authority (IANA), was the responsibility of Jon Postel at the University of Southern California.

World Wide Web

At the same time as these researchers were working on computer communications protocols in the United States, across the Atlantic Tim Berners-Lee was working as a telecommunications engineer in England solving the issues of type-setting software for computer printers.

In 1980, he accepted a contractor position at the European Center for Nuclear Research (CERN) in Geneva where he invented a way to facilitate the sharing of information among researchers through the concept of hypertext. After a short period away from CERN during which Berners-Lee worked in computer networking, he returned to CERN in 1984 as a fellow and had the inspiration to combine together hypertext, TCP/IP, and the domain name system to create the World Wide Web (WWW). The first website—info. cern.ch—went live in 1991 at CERN.

The excitement in the scientific and academic communities was intense as each person had their first experience of visiting new websites and reading the information stored on them. Before long there was a proliferation of new websites at academic and research centers around the world. The internet was born. However, it was far from easy to use.

Navigating the World Wide Web

In 1991, funding was allocated as part of the Gore Bill (introduced by then Senator Al Gore) to a new project called Mosaic, which would aim to make it easier to navigate the new World Wide Web. Marc Andreesen announced the project in 1993, and the first release occurred by the middle of the year. Andreesen would shortly leave the Mosaic project to create a commercial entity—Netscape Communications Corporation—that would launch the Netscape Navigator. This was the breakthrough that made the World Wide Web usable by anyone.

If browsers like Netscape made the World Wide Web navigable, users still needed to know where they were trying to get to: from all the world's online information, what would best solve the particular need they had at any given time? This required more than just an easy-to-use network and map. It required ways to search the information and identify the right places to visit for any given purpose.

The Search Engines

Before the first search engines were developed, the World Wide Web was indexed by hand. However, this became untenable as the explosion of content and websites hit the internet during the early- to mid-1990s.

Computer scientists at McGill University put their minds

together to finding a better way to search for content. Their invention, Archie, allowed for the creation of a searchable database of file names using directory listings located on the public anonymous File Transfer Protocol (FTP). Building upon this innovation, others then iterated to solve issues regarding classifying and searching the specific content held on websites. By 1993, Matthew Gray at MIT had developed the World Wide Web Wanderer, which cataloged the content of the web into an index called "Wandex." Wandex was followed in 1994 by WebCrawler that could search for specific words on any web page and then by the commercially successful Lycos search engine.

By the mid-1990s an increasing number of the general public were online searching the World Wide Web for information. In turn, this created more commercial viability for search engines. A plethora of contenders were launched, including AltaVista, Excite, Inktomi, Infoseek, Northern Light, and Yahoo! The competition between search engines became intense, and Netscape was able to sign deals with five of the contenders that agreed to be used in rotation by users of the Netscape search engine page.

During the dot-com boom of the late-1990s, search engines became one of the most highly valued areas for startups. We were investors in Excite and Inktomi, to name two, which we believed had enormous promise at the time.

Unfortunately for us, Sergey Brin and Larry Page built a better mousetrap with their PageRank innovation. This innovation allowed for more accurate search results based upon the backlinks that web pages had—the best sites appeared to be those that the largest number of other sites linked to for any specific topic.

And so—Google was born—and the search wars commenced in earnest with the eventual elimination of most other contenders. Yahoo! acquired Inktomi and Overture, which had meanwhile acquired AltaVista.

After working with AltaVista and Inktomi, Microsoft launched its own search engine, which is today Bing. By the mid-2000s, the Western world was served by only three principal search engines—Google, Yahoo!, and Bing—with regional solutions for Russia, China, and certain other specific purposes.

A Plethora of Communications Protocols

By the turn of the century, the core protocols of Ethernet, TCP/IP, and FTP had been joined by a plethora of other communications protocols created for specific purposes. Simple mail transfer protocol (SMTP), web transfer protocol (HTTP), voice over the internet protocol (VoIP), real-time transport protocol (RTP), and transport layer security (TLS/SSL) are just some of the more important examples.

All of these protocols had something in common: all were communications protocols built to make the fledgling internet work better at storing, finding, and sharing information.

None of these protocols was intended to be a commerce or financial protocol. They were created to allow communication over a worldwide network of computers. They were not created to enable worldwide commerce, financial transactions, payments, or any of the other types of human exchanges of value. These continued to be conducted off the internet in traditional financial and payments systems.

Five Big Issues the World Wants Resolved

This is not the only shortcoming of today's internet. As has been noted, it was not designed to be secure; initially, it was designed to be a wired network. As a result, today's wireless world suffers congestion in many ways. Through the process of competitive consolidation, it has become increasingly concentrated at every level in the hands of the winning companies—whether they be search engines, commerce providers, social networks, and so on.

Security, congestion, and concentration are three fundamental shortcomings of today's internet. They are challenges that need solving in the next manifestation of the internet that we will all use in our next-generation digital world.

However, the biggest shortcoming of all is the fact that today's internet is built upon communications protocols that do not easily support digital commerce. We cannot live in a digital world if we cannot conduct digital commerce at the same time as we communicate digitally. This implies not only that we need digital monies, but also that every asset that we have become digital.

In the remaining chapters of Part I of the book, we will look at the following five big issues in turn to see where our collective focus will be over the next two decades as we move the internet forward and complete the migration to a fully digital world. It is critical that we focus on these five issues because these will in turn become the drivers of the competitive dynamics of the next phase of the internet's evolution. Here are the five issues:

- Security
- Identity and Trust
- Concentration of Control
- Old-World Monies
- Old-World Assets

Those players that make the most progress in meeting the needs of every one of us, as reflected in this list of critical issues that we have today with the current state of our digital world, will secure a major part of the value that their solutions will unlock. Since we have already seen that the rollout of the current internet has already been the greatest value- and wealth-creation event ever, we can anticipate that this next phase will be just as instrumental in driving those monetary benefits.

In this chapter, we established that the digital revolution is far from complete. If the "next big thing" is upon us, we still need to have a view of what value proposition(s) we can make happen in its context. This means having a keen appreciation of the big issues that end users and society at large want to see resolved. Resolution of these issues is vital, for it will form the raw material from which powerful business visions and new value propositions can be built in the next phase. The next chapters focus on these five big unresolved issues.

Chapter 2
Security

A fool and his money are easily parted.

—Proverb

In this chapter, we look at the first of the five big issues that we all know we must solve—security. By understanding why the internet we have is so insecure, we begin to gain clarity on why the blockchain protocol may matter so much.

Frequent Massive Security Breaches

Billions of people are having key pieces of their online information stolen every year. The numbers are already massive and continue to grow quickly.

In a four-day period in 2018 Dunkin' Donuts, Marriott, and Quora all announced they had been breached. The Marriott breach was one of the largest ever, within the region of 500 million people losing their personal information stored in the Starwood guest reservation system. Data potentially stolen included guests' names, mailing addresses, phone numbers, email addresses, passport numbers, dates of birth, genders, arrival and departure information, reservation dates, and communication preferences. While the Quora breach "only" affected between 100 and 300 million users, the data accessed potentially included encrypted passwords along with those irritating questions and answers you are asked to respond to when your identity is being confirmed.

The biggest breach to date that we know of is the Yahoo! 2013 event in which as many as three billion accounts were accessed (Yahoo! had a second breach of 500 million accounts). Now there are only four billion people online, so even though many people have multiple accounts, we can see the magnitude of the security catastrophe we are living through.

We assume we are protected when we go online. We share our innermost behaviors, revealing our preferences, our opinions, the products we prefer and buy, and the services we use. Unfortunately, other people know us even better than we know ourselves.

Bad Actors/Bad Practices

The world is full of bad actors who conduct bad practices. This is nothing new. Since humanity began its time on earth, there was always a malevolent player trying to hurt us or encourage us to do something we were not supposed to. The only issue is that now the metaphorical snake in the grass is fully technologically enabled and is part of a global system of others who collaborate to take advantage of us, our families, and our businesses.

There are so many scams being played out that we can't begin to detail them in this book. However, to give you a flavor, let's talk about a common one—phishing. Phishing is an automated attack in which we are manipulated into giving up our data by online communications that look real but which are not.

How does phishing work? Let's look at the least complex

version—email phishing. First the phisher buys or steals a very large email address collection (there are marketplaces online in the dark web in which all those email accounts stolen from Yahoo! and others are sold to other bad actors). Let's assume our phisher bought as many as they could afford. Our phisher does not directly conduct breaches to obtain emails. Now the breacher prepares one or more communications, a fake web page is often created, and in the background a database is configured for the data, which is about to flow in. The breacher now sends out a wave of communications to the stolen email addresses. The fake message can be simple or very sophisticated. Often it will be modeled on the real messages we receive every day from our online providers. Next, we read the message and respond to it, filling out the fields in the popup windows, fake web pages, or forms.

The phisher may use the information they have gathered in a number of ways. Many just take it back to the dark web and sell it to others. Some make illegal purchases under the fake identities now in their possession. The really clever ones delay their campaigns and slowly leach away small amounts of money that we don't notice—sometimes over many years. Multiplied by the millions, five-dollar-a-year charges on one of your credit cards are going to go unnoticed, but will make them very wealthy.

Phishing has become a very large industry, and the internet that we rely upon in everything we do is now rife with very sophisticated bad actors who know how to apply very sophisticated bad practices to take advantage of us all. There are almost as many scams as there are legitimate uses of the internet, and the scale of the former is growing ever larger. This is why we so need to solve the issue of internet security.

Internet Not Designed for Security

Why is the internet not more secure? If the designers of the internet that we use every day had thought ahead, surely they would have embedded more secure capabilities into the platform we rely upon globally.

We touched on this in chapter 1. The designers of the internet, including Berners-Lee, Cerf, Kahn, Metcalfe, and all those other contributors at CERN, DARPA, MIT, SRI, and so on, were developing a communications platform, not a secure commerce platform. First, they were connecting computers together over wired networks—the address and identity of each computer was not in question. It was physically located in a major research center, visible to anyone who entered the computer lab. Second, they were making their own information available to other researchers. There was no risk of information being stolen. It was being made available freely just as scientists always broadcast their information into the academic communities in which they work. Third, they were not concerned about who stood behind each computer. Every computer connected together at the outset was operated by highly respected academic and scientific communities. There were no malevolent players on the network. Finally, there was no creative development of bad practices being perpetrated. The computers were just doing what they were programmed to do. Back then they had no ability to expand or improvise their programming. Artificial intelligence had not, and still probably has not, reached the point where computers can dissemble. They were just communicating.

As a result, the internet we have today is not very good at security. We really don't know who we are talking with online although we trust that the other end of any communication is with the person we thought we were interacting with.

We even trust that the packet of information we receive is the same as the one that started out on the trip to our device. We don't know that. We don't know that someone has not intercepted the communication, adjusted it, and sent it on to us in a modified and corrupted form. We trust that our global communications platform is secure, but in reality it is not because it was not designed to be.

What We Need Now

Now, as we move into the next phase of the development of our digital world, we need a secure commerce platform. This means we need protocols that establish security as a foundational principle, so it is embedded within the foundational layer of the internet rather than being added on top as an afterthought. Here are some dimensions of the characteristics that the new and more secure protocol must include: flows of data that are impossible to intercept and modify; immutable records of who did what with whom; fewer points of failure—at the extreme, billions of little nodes in a distributed network rather than hundreds of massive nodes in a centralized network inviting hackers to attack; much better ways to unveil bad actors when they do go to work; and incentives for every player in the network to work hard to ensure its integrity. With these secure protocols, everyone is on the watch and keen to stamp on the snakes once they appear.

It becomes even clearer that we still have a lot to do to evolve our internet forward when you consider the issues of identity and trust as we do in the following chapter.

Chapter 3
Identity and Trust

Trust, security, and service are even more important in a digital world.

—*Dan Schulman*

The second big issue with our internet is that of digital identity and the trust that is engendered when we know whom we are doing business with. In chapter 2, we showed how breaches allow others to steal or manufacture fake identities. However, we need to go deeper since commerce is built upon trust, which has typically been built upon knowing the other party.

A History of Trust

Most of our world has become increasingly connected over the last 200 years and in many ways is becoming more complex and more impersonal. In most communities, historically the constituent members of the group knew the other members. As we moved out of the "hunter-gatherer" era of tribal societies and into the "agrarian era" with its larger settlements and eventually cities, the concept that we knew everyone started to break down. But at least we knew whom we chose to do business with. We knew them by name, we knew them by face, we visited their places of commerce, and we handed our money into their hands over the counter.

Butcher, baker, candlestick-maker. Until relatively recently people conducted business with people they knew and trusted.

With the "mercantile era" and global trading we began to do commerce with others we had never, and probably would never, meet. Ships left port and sailed around the world, funded by merchants who expected to trade for goods that were valuable at home but that needed to be procured from distant lands. Sometimes a trusted family member was onboard to ensure the trade was fair and that we received the quality goods we had planned to buy. Sometimes we relied upon intermediaries that we believed to be trustworthy even if we had only recently met them as we placed out orders for the latest silks and laces inbound from the distant East.

Trust was the most important ingredient to make this work. As we substitute the physical commerce of the past with the online commerce of today and the future, trust has to pass onto new platforms and into digital form for us to be able to confidently do business this way. Indeed, we need trust more than ever since we know that a virtual world is full of unknown risks, as already established in the prior chapters.

In Those We Know, We Trust

In his excellent 2009 *Harvard Business Review* article, social psychologist Roderick Kramer lays out the basis for how we trust and describes seven rules for establishing trust. He outlines the thesis that human beings are designed to trust, it is built into our genes, and our childhood learning reinforces it. That trust is a survival mechanism that we rely upon to flourish in a dangerous world. From the day of our birth we are reliant upon others to survive, and we are engineered to be very good at building connections with those we need to care for us.

The basis of this trust is built upon identity. Within hours of birth we are looking into the eyes of those who hold us, and within days we are able to recognize the sound of our mother and father's voices. Tests have shown that once we can identify a face, we are more likely to say it is trustworthy even if we have no basis for no knowing if the other party can, in fact, be trusted. While we are engineered to tip towards trust, we only do so when we are sure of the identity of the other person. When the other person is a stranger, we are inclined to tip the other way into distrust. Identity leads first to trust in human relationships until we learn that the other is not trustworthy. As Kramer puts it, "Trust is our default position."

Not One But Many Identities

When most of us think about our identity, we tend to think first of the unchangeable descriptors: "I am an Asian man, aged 33, called John Smith, who resides at 1 Green Lane." However, this is only one way for us to describe our identity and in many cases not a very helpful way. Indeed, it is important that if we are looking to be trusted, that we view ourselves through the eyes of the other party rather than from our first-party perspective. When we do this, we begin to see the many possible identifiers that might be better employed in each situation. The reasons for this are several, which when taken together, compound to create many possible identities for each of us, such as the following:

- **Contextual**—the identity others want to know about depends upon the context in which they are looking to interact with us. So if we are going into an online site with restricted content, the operator may care about our age because they are regulated to ensure that underage visitors don't frequent their online store. On the other hand, when we ask to join an eSports team, they want to know if we are a good enough player to play with them. They don't care about our age per se but do care about our relevant capabilities.

- **Locally Defined**—what matters also varies by situation. For example, we have US drivers' licenses, so when we rent a car online for use in the US, it is all we need, along with a form of payment. However, in many countries, like, for example, Hungary, it is not recognized, so we can't rent a car online and use it there. We must get an international driving permit. The US driver's license is sufficient in some contexts but not in others.

- **Dynamic**—today we are accredited investors, and so if a seller of securities on a private investing platform online wants to offer us a US investment opportunity, that aspect of our identity will serve to qualify us. However, tomorrow we might lose all our money and cease to be accredited, in which case at that time our identity will no longer qualify us for investing with them.

- **Sufficient**—our identity has many descriptors, and there are many ways in which we are asked to prove our identity. Often this ends up making us reveal more than is necessary for the situation at hand. So, for example, if we reserve a hotel at an online travel service and then check in to the hotel, they may ask to see a passport at reception. However, that passport not only proves who we are, but it also includes our date of birth and where we have traveled, for example. The hotel does not need to know the latter, but the process of identification has revealed both more than they need and more than we would ideally offer them.

- **Ephemeral**—there are aspects of our identity that can't ever be taken away from us. Our age, for example. However, many aspects of our identity are attested to by third parties in order to be considered valid, and they may need constant third-party validation. So when we lose our passport, or if, for example, our country rescinds our citizenship, we may lose that aspect of our identity that was being used to prove our age. This may make it impossible for us to accomplish what we need until we can find a new party to provide us the attestation and act to validate us.

Taken together, these factors compound to create many different ways to think about a digital identity, many options for what we want to disclose in any context at any given time, and many options that others may want to see from us in order to trust and do business with us.

Externally- vs. Self-Administered Identity

Another important dimension of this issue of identity and trust is the question of who administers our digital identities. When we log in to an online service, for example, Gmail, we are asked to prove our identity through passwords. If we are able to remember them, the service accepts us and provides us access to work within its platform. When we log out, we cease to exist, at least in the eyes of Gmail at that time. Our information may remain in the platform, but we are no longer an active participant until we next log in. We can say that Gmail, in this case, is externally administering our identity with the help of other third parties. It has decided what descriptors of our identity are sufficient to proceed, it has decided where to store and manager those fields, and it decides when to allow us to be recognized.

Self-administered identity would work quite differently. We would control the aspects of our identity and decide what to share, with whom, and when. We might still rely upon third-party attestations, and the other party would need to let us know what aspects of our identity they consider sufficient to do business with us, but we would only show enough to proceed. At the extreme this concept is called self-sovereign identity, and a great deal of work is going into seeing whether it can be made workable in a digital world.

Internet Not Designed for Identity Management

As you can see, in our modern society most of us have many identities. While we are given a birth certificate with our name, date and location of birth, parents' information, etc., within days of life, that only serves a modest number of the future situations in which we will need to prove our identity and provide the attestations required to do business with others online. Indeed, even the birth certificate process is rife with identity theft and fraud as bad actors use fake birth certificates to manufacture whole new and made-up personalities.

When we get a little older, our governments may assign us social security numbers, passport numbers, tax identification numbers, and other identifiers to make us distinguishable from others. Theoretically, these numbers are unique and are with us for life. However, they have not ported well to the internet either. In some cases they have been used so frequently that in practice they have lost their purpose or have been overexposed.

Meanwhile, identify theft has skyrocketed. It seems that every day someone has created a fake account under our name—as when Matthew recently discovered he had a Saks credit card when he had never applied for one—or used our identity for some unknown purpose—as when Alison discovered that someone brazenly walked into a local jail and bailed their friend out of prison using her likeness.

Meanwhile, the internet we have has a variety of identity mechanisms built into it, but they are for computers, networks, and packets of data. It does not have any way of identifying the humans that are behind the computers. Without it, we can't trust the online parties we do business with. We need some sort of immutable personal identifier upon which the elements of trust can be placed: what we have done in the past; what we are good for in the future; what others should be comfortable doing with us; and where they are misplacing their trust because we are not the right ones to conduct that particular form of commerce with because we can't afford it, we can't be trusted to pay back, or it is not the right transaction for us to be a counterparty to. Perhaps that new digital identity can also be made smarter, and we can have more control over it—self-administered by each of us and able to minimize what we reveal about ourselves to each of the third parties that we wish to interact with.

What We Need Now

So what do we need as we move into the next phase of the development of our digital world?

We need reliable virtual identities upon which we can build trust. Some dimensions must include:

- Unalterable identities of ourselves online—as many as we need to get our goals met
- Portability so that we can take our identity(ies) with us wherever we go
- Ways to attach attestations to identities so that we know what a given identity is good for
- Ability to selectively share out identities with others so that we are not always 100% in plain view, but we get to control who sees what, and when
- Self-administration if possible

Again this is a very different list of attributes than our internet possesses today. Lasse Klassen, Founder of 1kx, underlines the opportunities that providing trust will open up when he says, "The killer feature of blockchains is trust. Investing thought into where and how, which institutions and people are making money for providing trust, and how they can be replaced with public blockchains, should have the highest ROI." Sidebar 2 provides an example of an initiative focused on providing an identity solution for our new digital world.

Sidebar 2: globaliD

Hard Yaka in San Francisco, the company created by serial entrepreneur and investor Greg Kidd, who backed Twitter, Square, Coinbase, and Ripple, among others, is taking on the task of creating a new—fit-for-a-digital-world—identity system with globaliD (GID). Greg explains the vision as follows, "globaliD enables people, rather than companies or countries, to own their identities as a basic right and responsibility. Properly implemented, our self-sovereign identities don't need to trade off privacy versus security. These values can be complementary rather than competing, with a payoff that all our permissions in life can be easier to access and more trusted."

GID enables each person or entity to own names that are a secure, private, and trusted means of controlling their assets and permission-based conduct. Specific names (or tokenized versions of those names) are unique across all use cases and legal jurisdictions in the world. The "portability" of authorization enabled by names means that third parties are no longer required to collect or store personally identifiable information (PII) to interact safely with GID users.

Each GID identity includes attestations from third parties who vouch for the authenticity of identity attributes at a particular point in time. Presentation of some (secret) attributes associated with an identity constitutes authorized access by the presenting party to act on behalf of the identity in question. Such action may involve the transfer of virtual and material property and/or permissions to engage in particular conduct. Conversely, others may transfer virtual or material property to, and conduct actions directed at particular identities, based on the belief that these destinations accurately represent the person or entity behind the identity in question. In summary, the project holds that:

- globaliD believes identity is the permission to act.
- While there are scores of identity providers, globaliD is unique in its focus on putting portable identity to work alongside, and eventually as a replacement for, traditional top-down, siloed identity solutions.
- That's because globaliD believes owning your own identity is a basic human right—a right and responsibility that rests with each of us, rather than something that is delegated from a country or a company.
- globaliD welcomes and enables all to a world in which our identity is defined by trusted interactions with one another. Such trust allowed ancient tribes to organize their social, economic, and political relations on a small scale without the need for technology. globaliD allows the same trust to manifest, but through infrastructure that scales globally, neutrally, and inclusively for every person and entity.

Sources: globaliD white paper and websites.

Players that are able to build visions of new businesses and value propositions that solve the global identity and trust issue will find an enormous world of new opportunities become possible with all of the implications for value creation. The next chapter explores whether these will be centralized or decentralized players.

Chapter 4
Concentration of Control

The American people should be made aware of the trend toward monopolization of the great public information vehicles and the concentration of more and more power over public opinion in fewer and fewer hands.

—*Spiro T. Agnew*

The third issue that we need to address as we move the internet forward is that it was not intended to be a centralized or heavily concentrated network.

Part of the original remit that DARPA was working towards was to create a crisis-tolerant computer system that would be able to withstand unexpected events like natural disasters and, of course, war. Decentralization was a central principle at that time because a failure in part of the system would be manageable if the rest of the system could continue to operate. Similarly, each end point (computer) on the network was meant to be able to communicate with each other end point in a fully connected network—communications did not ever need to go through a central computer, which could also become a single point of failure.

Connecting all the computers on a network also required interoperability. That is to say, computers designed and manufactured by different companies and running on different operating systems would need to be able to talk with each other. This was the central challenge for the original designers and led to the interoperable communications protocols that we have talked about in prior chapters.

However, things began to depart from these design principles as soon as the internet began to commercialize.

Commercialization Resulted in Concentration

In every area of technology that we have seen emerge over the last 40 years, the pattern has always been similar. First we see a few pioneers, next a plethora of wannabes, and then a shakeout, often accompanied by consolidation and feature acquisition, with the eventual emergence of a handful of large and capable competitors. The mainframe wars, the operating system wars, the search and browser wars, the mobile operating system wars, and so on, prove this observation. As the battle heats up, ever-larger players compete with each other; as they do so, they gain share and the activity in their respective space gets concentrated.

In the internet, the internet service providers (ISPs) began to battle first with early players, like AOL moving quickly to squeeze out smaller players. Microsoft made some early and powerful moves too: they added functionality into their Windows operating system, which had become the dominant software in the personal computer space, first by adding Internet Explorer to kill off Netscape and next by adding internet access to begin to displace independent ISPs.

Just as Microsoft started to pull ahead, Google surfaced with a much better search engine, which was able to wrestle away the access point that many users preferred for beginning their internet journeys. Search became the preeminent and cross-platform access point for the internet, and Google began its own rise to dominance squeezing out a plethora of other search engine providers in the process.

But it was not only operating software systems that led to concentration. The leading device manufacturers and the proprietary platforms that they developed also became a point of competition and concentration. From many, a few rose to dominance. Apple, Google's Android, the Wintel alliance, and a few overseas competitors, like Samsung, began to pull ahead. As a result, most device manufacturers had no choice but to throw in the towel on proprietary approaches and, instead, ally under the umbrella of one or a number of the dominant platforms.

Data was another point of competition. As we began to move to a mobile device and access model, so too we saw the rise of social platform players, like Facebook in the West and Tencent and Baidu in the East. In more commercially-oriented activities, Amazon, eBay, Apple, and Google in the West pulled far ahead of their smaller online competitors. In the East Alibaba effectively did the same.

Before we knew it, the once open-and-easy-to-launch-in internet became the domain of a handful of massive players.

With Market Share Came Market Value

It is not a coincidence that with this rise to prominence of a handful of very large centralized internet players came also a rapid escalation of market value in their hands. In prior decades the most valuable companies in the world were the largest energy companies, financial institutions, state-owned enterprises, and utilities. Today that is no longer true. The most valuable companies in the world are Amazon, Alphabet, Apple, Facebook, and Microsoft while Alibaba, Tencent, and others are not far behind.

This is not just because these companies are very profitable. It is also because the world's investors expect that these companies will continue to grow quickly and that their roles in the digital economy of the future will afford them the opportunity to capture enormous profit pools. Today's leaders are expected to become even stronger in a larger, and perhaps more centralized, future internet.

Political Concentration Also a Risk

It is not only commercial activities that become concentrated as control is accumulated. This may also give rise to points of failure and other potential risks.

Sovereign governments are, of course, in the business of providing leadership and governance for their peoples, and in the normal course of events that should be beneficial. However, political concentration of control becomes a risk for a country's people when the government becomes destabilized and/or moves away from focusing on the wellbeing of its people. Once a connected digital economy is added into the mix, this concentration of control at the governmental level can quickly become a point of potential failure or new risks. Some dimensions of this topic include the following four:

One—Insecure and Untrustworthy Monies

Some countries have economic systems that are not reliable at all. Countries that experience regular bouts of hyperinflation or modest rates of debasement compounded over a long time have populations that no longer trust the monies that their countries print. Countries like Argentina, Greece, Venezuela, and Zimbabwe are a few examples in which trusting in your savings in your local bank on a Friday turned out to be a big mistake on Monday.

These are not isolated examples. Some sources estimate that of the world's population as many as two billion people live in countries where their savings may be threatened by potential hyperinflation. Others believe that every sovereign-issued fiat money has been suffering a processing of continual debasement since the world left the gold standard in the 1970s.

Two—Political Destabilization and/or Expropriation

If a rapid or continuous decline in fiat money value is not sufficient reason to be concerned about how political concentration can lead to points of failure in a digital economy, there are also the issues of national destabilization and expropriation. If you live in a country, which may, for whatever reason, become destabilized, then the concentration of the digital economy and monies in its hands becomes a significant risk to you. If there is the prospect that you may be fleeing for your life with little or no warning, then you don't want all your wealth in a money that may be taken away from you at the border as you seek to leave.

Three—Sovereign Conflict

A concentrated digital economy is also at risk in terms of sovereign-level conflict. Ever since the Cold War we have seen nations researching how to undermine other nations in times of war by attacking the digital aspects of their opponents. Whether this means hacking and crashing a national geo-positioning system, undermining a country's trading and commerce platforms, or more subtly influencing a nation's political process, the concentration of the digital economy into systems that drive an economy and which may be managed in a centralized way by governmental (or private) agencies also raises the risks of failure in times of conflict.

Four—Data Misuses

A fourth way in which the concentration of the digital economy in sovereign hands can create risks and threats is with regard to "misuses" of personal data. "Misuses" is a subjective issue, and one person's greatest fear may be another's greatest hope. However, we are seeing the data flows that come from a unified digital economy being accumulated and put to new uses by governments that may in turn represent future risks that we are not fully appreciating today.

For example, a country can monitor all digital activities of their population, analyze and assess that data, and create social scores of who is doing what where. Then if they can also manage their entire economy with a digital money that they control, they can combine the two to take actions depending upon what they find. This could, on the one hand, be powerful in furthering the beneficial work of government. However, on the other hand, it could be used to control or manage citizens in very powerful ways that override any notion of individual freedom and choice. For example, governments might "turn off" the purchasing power of individuals that they deem disruptive or bad behaving, and conversely they might open up "attractive goods" to those who show the behaviors that they most value and wish to accentuate.

Taken together, most of the world's population is exposed to these types of risks of political concentration in the digital economy, including insecure and untrustworthy currencies, the risks of national political instability and/or expropriation, actions that might be orchestrated in times of sovereign conflict, and the potential for data-based actions aimed at individual freedoms.

Failure Points Becoming Critical

Centralization is not all a bad thing. The internet has grown rapidly, costs have come down enormously, and "free" is often the preferred model for everything from information access, to entertainment, to communication. Everyone has benefitted from this time of unprecedented innovation, and the largest internet players have provided much of this innovation and consumer value.

The reason that Alibaba and Amazon are growing so fast is that consumers find them preferable to traditional retail options in terms of choice, cost, speed, and service. Michael Porter in his groundbreaking books *Competitive Strategy* and *Competitive Advantage* taught us to choose a vector of competition. These internet giants have competed on all of the major competitive dimensions at once and in some cases have beaten their traditional competitors on every level simultaneously.

The cons are real too. Centralization can lead to monopoly power and certainly gives rise to central points of failure as our earlier chapter on security illustrated. From a national security perspective, this is of fundamental concern. Future wars will be based upon the ability to disrupt, deflect, and control the digital world, and centralized systems make that a scary proposition. Of course, bad actors love being able to hack, steal, and damage large chunks of activity all at once. If you are going to take the risk of being an illegal actor, you want the payoff to be as large as possible, and centralized systems provide that opportunity.

What We Need Now

We need fault-tolerant systems, for sure, and we want the benefits of scale and scope without the risks of over-concentration and control in the hands of a few. How exactly we square that circle is unclear at this time.

Recently, a movement has surfaced that argues that returning to a distributed internet with a decentralized architecture is the solution. On paper that seems to have merits, but we have yet to see a fully commercial and effective implementation of a decentralized internet. Will it work? We are not sure.

We watch with concern as recent decentralized projects have quickly become controlled by a few who have used them to corner the market on the value created. Conversely, as investors, that is always our mission—to invest and capture a disproportionate share of the value that innovation unleashes.

From a competitive strategy perspective, this is the one among the five big issues that is less clear at this time. While any player that establishes a viable vision and strategy for solving security and identity and trust in the internet is going to meet with enormous opportunity, the issue of whether the internet is better centralized or decentralized is likely to continue to be a debate for some time, we expect. In the next chapter, we turn to the fundamental issue of how a truly commercial internet can be created once we have native digital monies.

Chapter 5
Old-World Monies

The one thing that's missing, but that will soon be developed,
is a reliable e-cash, a method whereby on the internet you can
transfer funds from A to B, without A knowing B or B knowing A.

—*Milton Friedman*

The fourth big issue for the internet in this timeframe is that it still relies upon old-world monies. Milton Friedman provided a clear perspective on this 20 years ago when he pointed out that we are missing a reliable e-cash. He was certainly correct in his observation, but he was off on the timing—as is so often the case with disruptive technologies and innovations. Every type of monetary transaction today could benefit from the introduction of native digital monies.

The Functions of Money

There are three functions of money in any economy—unit of account, medium of exchange, and store of value.

Unit of account means that money allows us to compare the value of other items in a common and easily understood way. We price goods and services in dollars, pounds, or other currencies, and then know the relative prices of each. We hope that the monetary unit that we are using as unit of account will maintain its value, but even if it does not, the items we wish to compare will have a common measure to allow comparison. We then use that money to effect transactions as a medium of exchange. Finally, we may store the money and use it in some future period.

In this chapter, we deal with aspects of money as a unit of account and a medium of exchange. We will do so by exploring retail online commerce although this is only one of many use cases for money in our evolving digital economy. In the next chapter, we will focus on money as a store of value.

A World of Internet Payments

Right now more than four billion people are connected to the internet. While it began as a research initiative in Europe and the US, today the majority of global internet users are in Asia, with China representing the largest online market of all. China has over 750 million internet users while the US is third with slightly less than 300 million. While the US has higher penetration of its population using the internet, reflecting its greater affluence, China is coming on fast and from a commerce perspective leads in many ways. Despite this, English is the common language of the internet.

We noted in chapter 1 that the internet was originally designed as a wired network between computers. Today the internet has gone mobile. From email, to online search, to video and commerce, most users—and the vast majority of young users—rely upon their mobile devices for their internet access and usage.

Statista estimates that in 2018 e-commerce accounted for US $2.8 trillion of worldwide revenue and that this will double by 2021 to US $4.9 trillion. In terms of global mobile e-commerce, Statista also estimates that in 2018 almost US $700 billion will be spent by consumers, with the highest penetration rates on consumer online spending in Asia. We all know the names of our favorite online retailers—Alibaba, Amazon, Apple, Google, Tencent, and so on.

For many, online commerce is an everyday occurrence while going to the mall or supermarket has become a once-a-week, at most, trip. With in-home devices, like Alexa and Google Assistant, and artificial intelligence-driven interfaces, like Alexa, Hey Google, and Siri, it is becoming easier and more convenient to buy through your internet-connected device and take delivery at home or anywhere else in the world that you tell them to ship to.

We all buy and sell things every day on the internet. Most of us just assume that when we do so, we are completing the entire transaction online—we are not.

How Does It Really Work?

When we shop online, we fully leverage the key characteristics of the internet. We can go online anywhere in the world, from any connected device, log in to our accounts at our favorite online retailer, or search free-form for what we want to buy in a search engine, conduct our research, compare prices, select our choice, and click "buy."

When we do so, in split seconds we receive back some sort of communication from the seller. If it is a large online player, like Amazon, the response is usually a confirmation that the order has been accepted and that we should see an email or message with the details of our purchase and likely delivery dates. Since 90% of us pay by some sort of card—debit or credit—in Western markets, our account will be billed for our selection. If it is a digital good, like a book, piece of music or videogame, the purchase once completed is accompanied by access to either open the purchase, or perhaps initiate a download to our mobile device.

It is as simple as that. Just two parties, seller and buyer, coming together over the internet and completing their transaction completely online.

Actually—no, it is not that simple. Let's look again.

The communications between buyer (consumer) and seller (merchant) do go over the internet at almost real-time speeds. If the merchant has automated their end of the communication, as most have today, their response is coming back to the consumer in milliseconds. The consumer does the hard work—searching, researching, selecting, and asking to buy. The merchant end has by now been codified to give as-fast-as-possible service. In the past they may have needed to put up a few screens confirming purchase quantity, size, delivery address, method of payment, and so on, but even those might have been collapsed into a single screen if the consumer has a prior relationship with the retailer and has selected "one-click" buying.

But the financial aspects of this purchase are not completed online. Far from it.

Financial Payment Processes

Almost all of our financial payment methods that we rely upon today were created before the internet was really taking off in the 1990s. Even those that have been invented since, like China's Alipay or WePay, need to go through traditional payment processes and systems. Unlike the purchase communication, which just involved consumer and merchant, the payment process involves a host of intermediaries—often with significant cost when expressed as a percentage of the value of the transaction—especially if the transaction is a small one.

Consumer Side

To make this whole process work the consumer has used a payment product— most probably a credit or debit card in the US.

- **Issuer Bank**—the card has been issued by the consumer's own bank—the issuing bank. The credit and debit card bank issuers get paid "interchange"—which is the transaction fees charged to the merchant's bank account every time a customer uses their card to make a purchase. Interchange fees are paid to the card-issuing bank to cover handling costs, fraud and bad debt costs, and the risks involved in approving the payment. They also help pay for the "loyalty" programs—airline points, cash back, and other benefits—which incentivize people to use the cards in the first place.
- **Issuer Processor**—this is what companies like Fiserv and First Data do. They communicate with the issuing banks to authorize and settle debit and credit card transactions, which are in process on the merchant side.

The consumer pays a variety of fees and receives in return a variety of benefits beyond being able to pay for their purchase. While the annual fees for the card may appear modest, and some cards are free, there are many other fees that kick in especially if the consumer is not always able to pay or forgets to pay their monthly bill (especially on credit products). High interest rates, late payment fees, foreign currency spreads on international transactions, or automated teller transaction (ATM) fees are all examples, and each may also bring in other players.

Modern cards also have additional benefits to the consumer, including purchase insurance, card loss and fraud coverage, concierge services, the almost ubiquitous loyalty programs, such as those Matthew launched with American Express, Bank of America, Chase, and Gap over 25 years ago, and so on.

Most consumers like their payment methods, but very few are sufficiently analytical and/or disciplined to calculate the true cost of their ownership or the value of the benefits they actually use as compared to those that are offered to them.

Merchant Side

For the merchant, it is quite complex. At minimum they will have set up a number of things in order to become an online retail player, for example:

- **Merchant Account**—the merchant account is a type of bank account that accepts most major financial payment methods. Typically in the US, at minimum, the account will accept Visa, Mastercard, American Express, PayPal, and often e-checks and direct bank debits of various types for retail transactions. The merchant account is held at a bank that agrees to act as the merchant's representative (acquiring bank).

- **Acquiring Bank**—the bank that offers the merchant account agrees to manage the funds that flow as consumers transact with the merchant's online store, including the complexities that may result from cancelled purchases, returns, chargebacks, and other such interactions that may occur after the initial confirmation to buy has been made.
- **Merchant Payment Processor**—the payment processor assigns a unique merchant identification number (merchant ID) to the seller and to its merchant account. This is the unique ID that is needed for every payment that takes place on the merchant's website. The payment processor will then handle the verification and completion of the payment between the merchant's acquiring bank and the consumer's issuing bank. Examples of payment processors are Fiserv and First Data (where Alison is a board director), and newer players like PayPal, Due, Stripe, and so on.
- **Payment Gateway**—the payment processor will then provide a payment gateway to the merchant—sometimes bundled with their own services, sometimes from another independent player. This is the online equivalent of a point-of-sale (POS) terminal. It is software that, once connected to the merchant's online store and their merchant account, can provide a number of services.

For working with a payment gateway and a payment processor, a merchant pays a variety of fees including interchange fees, merchant acquirer processing fees, monthly statement fees, application and set-up fees, monthly minimum fees, monthly gateway access fees, and early termination fees. The total fees charged can vary widely but can be as high as 2.5 to 5% of the value of the transaction being made—and even more for small transactions.

Card Associations/Payment Networks

Between the consumer side and merchant side of the transaction lie the payment rails, the card associations and the payment networks they manage. To keep it simple, the payment processor communicates with the card association for the payment process that the consumer selected. If the consumer uses a Visa card, as an example, Visa receives a communication from the payment processor that a transaction is in process. Visa then asks for authorization from the consumer's issuing bank that the consumer is good for the transaction. If the response is yes, Visa responds back to the payment processor with a transaction confirmation that flows back through the payment gateway to the merchant who can then send a communication to the consumer that indeed they can buy that item they had their eyes on.

Credit Approval/Fraud Players

For those purchases that require it—large value items or transactions in which the consumer plans to use credit—other activities are added to the payment process, and sometimes other players come into the game.

As an example, the major payment networks (Visa, Mastercard, American Express) have in-house data that allows them to pre-approve many transactions, but these databases may be updated with input from credit rating agencies who can look across the consumer's transactions and report examples of non-payment or late payment that may be occurring outside the "on-us" activities of the network in question. This sharing of data is critical to ensure that large transactions are not processed on one network while the consumer is in default on another.

New Payment Players

The process outlined above is not without innovation of course. Relatively recently we have seen the development of third-party payment processors who don't create a unique merchant account for each merchant that they do business with. Instead they consolidate a larger number of merchants into one merchant account and keep track of which merchant has been responsible for each transaction through software. This innovation has reduced some costs, especially where the transaction is fully online. However, even the processes of PayPal, Due, Braintree, and others occur off the internet.

The payment gateways have also been subject to innovation. On the one hand, technology-enabled electronic POS providers like Clover—now owned by First Data—are providing better integration into a company's customer and operational data collection and analysis solutions, so that, for example, merchants can know who spent what and where, allowing them to run more targeted and effective campaigns and promotions, and allocate their hours, staffing, and stock to better match demand.

In turn, this has given rise to new technology-enabled payment, loyalty, and marketing providers that run on electronic POS. In the UK Yoyo wallet is a case in point (Sidebar 3). The integration of real-time payments, consumer data, and merchant offers has made Yoyo a very attractive solution to UK customers and merchants like Caffè Nero and Planet Organic. In the US, software-as-a-service (SaaS) loyalty solutions like Perkville are also examples of what can be accomplished once the POS is fully digital and can track consumer activity more effectively.

Mobile device providers like Apple and Google Android have built pay-by-phone capabilities into their mobile devices, which allow consumers to tap and pay at enabled merchants. To the consumer this seems like magic. Payments that occur at the wave of a hand. However, don't be fooled. The payment process that takes place on the merchant side is not much different from the traditional flow outlined above: it does not occur over the internet, and it involves many players and many costs.

Sidebar 3: Yoyo

Founded in 2013, Yoyo's mission is to disrupt the world of payment, transforming a transaction into a delightful, rewarding experience for shoppers. For retailers it offers a customer data-led engagement and marketing channel.

Delivering a complete omnichannel infrastructure, Yoyo integrates electronic point-of-sale (EPOS) payments, cards, loyalty, and one-on-one marketing programs to create a seamless point-of-sale experience for its 1.5 million users while harnessing individual basket data to provide customer-relationship management (CRM), business intelligence, and marketing tools. In this way, retailers can personally engage, reward, and retain their customers. As Michael Rolph, co-founder and CEO of Yoyo, puts it, "Every high street brand vies for a consumer's attention and must find ways to stand out from the crowd."

Yoyo provides a range of functionality integrated into one seamless offering:

- The world's most powerful data-led commerce platform—Yoyo helps retailers to capture customer-basket-data insight at the point of sale, understand their customers better, and deliver targeted marketing campaigns based on individual purchasing behavior.
- Payment, loyalty, rewards, and digital receipts in one—a single scan of a secure Yoyo-powered QR code enables instant payment, loyalty (points and/or stamp) collection and delivery of rewards, and an itemized digital receipt.
- Best-in-class digital loyalty programs—Yoyo allows retailers to choose what items are available to customers via their tailor-made loyalty program, they can pick their redemption rates, and they can measure the ROI of their activity.
- Personalized campaigns and experiences—Yoyo allows retailers an easy campaign setup and promotion via GDPR-compliant in-app messaging, push notifications, and email. All activity can be personalized around profile and purchase data, so

that campaigns can be set up against business goals.

- Referrals and sharing—retailers can grow their user base and spread some brand love among customers and their friends with Yoyo's referral and voucher-sharing mechanisms.

- Order ahead—with Yoyo retailers can offer a VIP experience and remove the customer's need to stand in line and wait. Yoyo allows customers to order and pay for food and drink in advance, leaving a simple pick-up of the ordered items.

- Customer feedback—Yoyo allows retailers to receive instant feedback from users without the typical effort and expense. Retailers can choose from an Uber-style star rating or a long form, multi-question format.

Given its ability to support the creation and maintenance of communities and enable integrated incentives systems, we see blockchain being integrated into new payment platforms such as Yoyo moving them even further ahead of traditional payment providers.

Source: Yoyo wallet website and press articles.

Native Digital Money: How It Might Work

As you can see, there is quite a bit of complexity and cost associated with turning that blindingly quick communication between buyer and seller into a completed financial transaction. Furthermore, very small microtransactions are not economical in today's system and don't make sense for the various parties to process. This is why we can't use traditional payment processes for, as an example, buying virtual goods in videogames that might cost a few cents each or compensating microtransactions that may be enabled by connected devices as part of the internet of things (IoT).

Cost, complexity, time to complete the transaction—all significant burdens on what was supposed to be an instantaneous low-cost online purchase and at a high cost to the merchants or sellers who bear the brunt of the costs.

In contrast, an internet with native digital monies would work very differently. There are many options for how it might work, but just consider this example.

Imagine that we have native digital money. You own some. It is stored in the internet with your rights to it clearly defined. Your digital identity allows only you to determine when and how to make it accessible to others. You want to buy a digital book from Amazon. You click the purchase button and send the communication that you want the item now, just as you do today. However, concurrent with and attached to that communication, Amazon receives a packet of software that includes a contract that surrounds the keys to own a portion of your digital money sufficient to complete the transaction. The software will unlock once Amazon completes the requirements of the contract—which in this case might be proof that the digital book you are buying has been delivered to you. Amazon accepts your request, confirms it back to you, completes its side of the transaction, the contract unlocks, and Amazon now owns the digital money instead of you. The entire transaction occurred within the internet. Unlike today, where the transaction communication occurs within the internet, but the commercial side of the transaction occurs outside the internet.

Benefits of Native Digital Money

While simplistic, the benefits of this approach are enormous relative to our payment system of today. The transaction can be almost cost-free, fully digital, and almost instantaneous if Amazon completes its obligations quickly—e.g., sends a digital copy of a book to your device. Notice too, many of the players are potentially no longer needed. We still have buyers and sellers and probably payment gateways. But perhaps the merchant acquiring banks, issuing banks, payment processors, and payment networks have all gone away, or play a very different role. So too the credit rating agencies. If a third party has attested that our communication contains sufficient digital cash within the contract, the risk of nonpayment and chargebacks for the merchant should have been greatly reduced. Or if these various players still exist, they will perhaps have become fully digital and much more efficient, given the relatively minor set of activities they would be required to complete.

First Experiments

This is not as new an idea as it may appear. As early as 1982, fintech innovator David Chaum published the idea of electronic money. He called it eCash, and his concept provided for a user to own and store money in a digital format on their computer, cryptographically authorized by a financial institution. Merchants would be able to receive this digital money if they agreed to accept eCash as a valid form of payment. No accounts, numbers, etc., were needed to make this work. Chaum made this possible with the use of public key digital signatures, which are still the principal innovation being applied in today's versions of eCash. Unfortunately, after almost 10 years of trying, Chaum's company DigiCash was only able to get one bank and a few thousand trial customers to experiment with eCash. The US experiment ended in 1998.

In Europe and in Asia, electronic cash has received more acceptance, and over 20 years leading banks, including Deutsche Bank, Bank Austria, Credit Suisse, Nomura, and others, have put in place e-cash solutions. However, as we have discussed already, the vast majority of online payments are still conducted through payment processes outside the internet, and the preferred payment method is the credit or debit card rather than native digital monies.

Institutional Payments

In this chapter, we have illustrated the complexity of today's financial payment system by focusing on the simple case of a retail purchase over the internet. There are tens of billions of such transactions every year, and VisaNet alone handles more than 150 million transactions every day and has the capacity to handle 24 thousand transactions per second. But when looked at through the lens of value of transactions, rather than number of transactions, this is swamped by the payment system that supports the activities of financial institutions, governments, and large corporations. The institutional payments world appears a complex web of players and old technology platforms created in the Industrial Era and repurposed for this new digital world in which we live today. The weight of financial costs, time of transactions, risks of fraud and cyber attack, and extra effort that result are significant just as in the retail payments world. It is just much much bigger in value terms. The payments world, retail and institutional, is far from having completed its digital revolution.

Sidebar 4 provides the example of Ripple and XRP that are working hard to build an interoperable solution to institutional international money transfers made with native digital monies.

Sidebar 4: Ripple and XRP

Ripple connects banks and payment providers via RippleNet to provide a frictionless experience for sending and receiving money globally. RippleNet is a product suite that enables financial institutions to transfer money globally, instantly, reliably, and for fractions of a penny. Through the use of blockchain and the digital asset XRP, financial institutions can immediately communicate information about a payment between each other in real time and settle the payment instantly. The technology provides interoperability with standard banking IT infrastructure and proprietary blockchains, which is the only possible way to deliver a truly frictionless global payments experience.

XRP, an independent digital asset for global payments, is faster, more efficient, and more scalable than other cryptocurrencies. XRP can be used by financial institutions to lower costs associated with cross-border payments. Payments into emerging markets can require using correspondent banks or pre-funded local currency accounts at the destination, which can be costly and slow. Instead, payment providers and banks can use XRP to fund these payments on-demand, without intermediaries.

Ripple has already proven a viable competitor to existing financial services infrastructure and business models built on SWIFT. Ripple has more than 200 customers across all types of financial institutions, including banks and payment providers. RippleNet is powering cross-border payments to over 40 countries across six continents.

Ripple was co-founded by Chris Larsen and Jed McCaleb in September of 2012. XRP and XRP Ledger were created by Jed McCaleb, Arthur Britto, and David Schwartz in early 2012.

Recently, we are beginning to see large financial institutions, governments, and regulators realize that this issue of native digital monies can be transformative. As just one example, JPMorgan has announced the creation of its own proprietary digital money called JPM Coin, which will be used to settle payments between the bank's clients and possibly enable international cross-border payments as well as having a role in tokenized corporate debt offerings. This is a fascinating development given that the bank's leader, Jamie Dimon, is reported to have spoken out about "the fraud that is bitcoin" just a few months earlier.

What We Need Now

Native digital monies for a fully digital world.

The accelerating proliferation of projects and players focused on bringing native digital monies into existence is clear evidence that we are entering a competitive phase around resolving this big issue. Governments, large financial institutions, and a host of disruptive projects and companies are all attacking this issue. Additionally, there are already almost certainly more potential digital monies than the world needs. Figuring out how to capture competitive advantage for your initiative is key.

However, in the next chapter we turn from monies to assets and show that there is perhaps an even larger opportunity to also resolve the way that every asset, as well as every transaction, can become digital in this next phase of the internet evolution. If we need native digital monies why would we not also need a similar innovation for the way we record, store, and transact value in the form of other assets that are also claims on value?

Chapter 6
Old-World Assets

Almost any illiquid asset today lends itself well to becoming tokenized. It will create a deeper market with improved price discovery and should increase the value of those assets.

—David O. Sacks

The fifth big issue for the continued evolution of the internet in this timeframe is the creation of native digital assets. The case for native digital assets is very similar to that for native digital monies. The deadweight loss of the complex, manual, often paper-based ways in which we track and trade real-world assets is enormous. There are no asset classes where the benefits of making their ownership, trading, and transfer fully digital would not be enormous.

Past Is Prologue

Back in the 1980s, we were business analysts at McKinsey & Company in London working for financial institution clients confronted by the "Big Bang." This was the process of financial deregulation that had been unleashed by Margaret Thatcher, the prime minister at the time. The abolition of fixed commission charges and the introduction of technology-enabled trading moved the stock exchange off the physical trading floor. Instead of stock-jobbers and stockbrokers shouting at each other in a cacophony of noise called "open outcry," trading was technology enabled such that computers could communicate directly with other computers to initiate and settle trades. The computers were fast, with almost infinite capacity, and allowed ever-narrower spreads and costs.

By the mid-1990s almost all public equities were being traded electronically. By the 2000s, when Alison was CFO and head of strategy at Barclays Global Investors (which was the largest investor in public equities globally and is now part of Blackrock), it was inconceivable that open outcry could be an effective way to make investment transactions or that paper could still be the primary way to effect trades.

However, in many investment and asset markets there has not yet been a Big Bang moment.

Global Stores of Value

There are a lot of ways to store value in our global economy. Some are ancient—precious stones like diamonds and rubies, precious metals like gold and silver, works of art and other collectibles. Human beings have always treasured these as ways to store their wealth. And we still do today.

However, those are not the big global stores of value in our modern world. Physical commodities like gold, silver, platinum, oil and so on, are the oldest ways of storing wealth and are still used today. Gold is probably the most important and has a worldwide value of around US $7 trillion at the current price of US $1,300 per ounce as we are writing this book.

Moving up the scale to larger stores of value—physical cash comes next, with all the notes in circulation around the world having a value of perhaps US $25 trillion. As we have noted before, unlike physical commodities, government-backed monies can be issued at will and almost all have been continuously debasing since the world moved off the gold standard. This happened in the 1970s when President Richard Nixon announced a temporary closing of the gold window—which has not been reopened since, such that the gold standard has, in practice, ceased to exist.

The world's listed public equities—all the company securities bought and sold on stock exchanges and through computerized trading globally—have a combined value of about US $57.5 trillion. The Big Bang applied technology to the trading of those assets. These securities are now part of the digital economy.

The next largest tracked asset class is investable/tradable real estate (or property, for our European readers) at US $70 trillion. This is greater than the combined value of the world's listed public equities. However, this is only "investable" real estate. There is also a world of real estate that is not traded on marketplaces, so it does not get into the asset numbers being reported above. These are the myriad of private real-estate holdings that are invisible to the world's public markets.

Most of the world's real estate is not traded electronically. With the exception of certain large portfolios of properties that may be bundled together and sold on exchanges (for example, real-estate investment trusts or REITs in the US), most of this land and the buildings built upon it are traded in old-fashioned ways. They use paper-based processes, which are inefficient, time-consuming, and hard for investors to leverage for active and high-velocity investing.

Even greater than gold, cash, public equities, and real estate is global debt—national and local government bonds, corporate bonds, securitized loans. It is huge and growing rapidly and was estimated to be US $175 trillion in 2018.

The last major store of value that we can measure accurately is made up of derivative assets. The derivatives markets are staggeringly large at more than US $700 trillion, of which the vast majority are interest rate-related at US $577 trillion. These are massive investment marketplaces. Some are for good purpose, like when a corporation wants to hedge against a possible future move in interest rates that might harm it. However, most of the trading that takes place on these derivatives markets is speculation. Some would say the derivatives markets are mostly massive gambling casinos that add no real value to the world's economy. They don't launch businesses, build buildings, hire people, or create new products and services. They just trade to make (and lose) money—in massive volumes, with attractive fees for the bankers and market makers who facilitate them.

There is another important asset category—global private equity—that is hard to measure because it is not traded or easily tracked as a store of wealth. This is a broad category because it includes large private companies like those that are family-owned (e.g., Bechtel, Cargill, and Koch Industries) and those that are rapidly growing towards a public offering (e.g., Airbnb). It is the domain of very large funds measured in the tens and hundreds of billions of US dollars. For example, KKR, Oaktree, and TPG that put billions of dollars to work every year buying and selling private businesses. However, this category also includes every small business or sole proprietorship in the world of which there are hundreds of millions globally.

Most of these private companies have issued securities and have investors on their corporate capitalization tables—even if those investors are only the founders themselves. These tables record the ownership of the company—typically on spreadsheets held by the company or its lawyers. Each constituent security is usually written down on paper and saved on private computer drives with no visibility to external parties, let alone technology-enabled marketplaces.

Most private equities have not begun to enter the realm of our digital world. This poses a challenge because every country in the world believes that small businesses, especially the start-up innovation ecosystems, are the drivers of jobs and gross domestic product. Every country in the world wishes to cultivate and stimulate entrepreneurs and the companies they launch, but has limited ways of encouraging capital to flow to this asset class. Because governments and institutional investors focus on the organized investment markets—cash, listed equities, and debt—we don't know the stored value of private equities. Even still, in the sections that follow we will explore how this world works today.

Early-Stage Technology Investing Example

Let's focus on one specific store of value that is not yet digitized to see how it works and how it might be brought into early-stage technology investing—a sub-part of private equity investing—both to see how the digital revolution has impacted it and to see what work still remains to be done for us to truly have a digital economy.

In the US there are more than 30 million small (private) businesses employing approximately 60 million people. Those businesses added a net two million jobs to the economy in 2015 when the US Small Business Administration last counted. Most of those jobs—1.1 million—were in turn added by small businesses with less than 20 employees.

Of these small businesses some are early-stage technology startups. We know that early-stage investors—often called angel investors—back more than 70 thousand companies a year in the US with more than US $22 billion—this money flows into the formation and seed rounds. Venture capital firms (VCs), on the other hand, that typically invest when the companies are more advanced—the Series A round or later—backed more than 5,500 companies with almost US $100 billion in capital. However, almost all of the VC investment occurred in the later stages of the private companies' lifecycle in fundraising rounds of US $100 million and up. This was historically called growth or expansion capital rather than early-stage venture capital.

For the purpose of this example, let's assume that each year around 70 thousand early-stage technology companies are being funded in the US—but we don't know the cumulative "stock" of these securities since that is not tracked. How does this early-stage technology investing work?

Form of the Security

The security that is being sold can be almost anything that the entrepreneur and their lawyers want to create and sell. While in general there are some typical parameters for the security that will be created for the formation round (common stock), the seed round (seed preferred stock), the Series A (Series A preferred stock), and so on, the specifics can vary enormously. In addition, early-stage technology companies may issue notes (SAFEs, convertible notes, etc.), share options, warrants, and a plethora of other securities.

The process of creating each security is typically multi-stage. For example, very generally, it can play out like this:

- Entrepreneurs sit down with their lawyers and decide what terms and conditions they would like.
- Next they talk to investors who may take out a red pencil and edit and revise the security under consideration.
- After some back and forth, which may be iterated as other investors come to the table, everything will eventually converge on an agreed investment security.
- The lawyers will then write this up as a contract that both sides will sign.
- Paper copies will be printed out and filed, and paper certificates may be mailed.
- In practice, digital copies will also be filed and in some cases will need to be sent to regulators who keep track of what is being issued and to whom.

Of course it is much more complicated than that, depending upon jurisdiction, type of offering company, type of investor, and so on. But the big point is that it is paper-based, highly customized, not very transparent, and with lots of expenses throughout the process. Certainly not digitally enabled.

Capitalization Tables

Once the security has been agreed upon, and the money has changed hands from investor to company, then everything needs to be recorded. The place within the company that these matters are held and updated over time is the company capitalization table (cap table). In the past this was literally a paper ledger, which recorded purchases and sales of each of the securities that would be issued during the life of the company. As a newly minted McKinsey business analyst, Matthew was once given the task of summing up all of the investments that had been made by one of England's most active early-stage investors—Electra—and it was often quite difficult to read the handwriting of what warrants, options, and shares had been purchased and sold.

The rights and privileges of each specific security are not recorded on the cap table. However, by reference to the cap table, and with access to folders and files, it is possible to find out who owns what. All of this has moved to electronic spreadsheets in most situations today. However, nothing is integrated together so that manual entries are relied upon. Yet when needed, including as a company prepares for a subsequent funding round, or even a public offering, a company finance person, or a paralegal at a law firm, will be able to figure out the overall ownership of the company. In theory.

Unfortunately, we rarely see clean cap tables in the world of early-stage technology investing. Things get recorded but then things change. Options are granted but never vested because people leave the firm before the vesting term of their grants. Investors pass on, sell, or split their holdings, but either forget to tell the company or tell the company but the latter forgets to update the cap table. Deaths, divorces, bankruptcies, and so on, happen, and the implications for multi-round investment commitments or holdings don't get properly recorded. Or manual entry errors simply occur.

That is all before you need to consider the international implications of companies raising money from investors in other jurisdictions where the rules may be quite different concerning what can be sold and who can buy it. Such that the cap table may not only be wrong. It may actually be recording things that are not allowed by law.

We have rarely seen an early-stage technology company cap table without problems—which has enormous consequences for trying to apply technology to enabling investment activities.

Primary Issuance Investment Rounds

Digging just a little deeper into this, it is worth taking a look at a typical investment round.

We have already noted that the security being sold is custom and iterates during the course of the round. The potential investor ranks are changing even more rapidly during the course of an investment round.

Typically, a company's founders and executives need to pitch to at least 10 times as many investors as they will eventually receive funds from. Sometimes the ratio is closer to 100 to 1. In many cases, the entrepreneur will pitch to vast numbers of investors and never raise anything at all.

This dance of fundraiser with investor is mostly happening in person and/or by electronic communication. Emails, telephone calls, online webinars, and so on, get used to make the pitch and to answer the resulting questions. What is said becomes hearsay in most cases since often it is not recorded. The formal documentation of the investment will take place as the lawyers work on behalf of their clients, but all the plans, predictions, forecasts, and expectations that led to the investor being convinced don't go into the folders that hold the investment security. Thus, most are lost forever.

No Liquidity

In most asset classes, making an investment is just the beginning of the process. You plan to sell at some point in the future, and in many markets the sale happens very fast indeed. We have talked about computer-based trading and derivatives markets. In many asset classes the store of value is constantly being bought and sold. This is called liquidity. For the most part highly liquid markets are good things. They help provide pricing, make sure buyers and sellers can make a trade when they want to, and make the market more efficient since the liquidity flows towards those who will make the trades at the lowest costs.

In early-stage technology investing there is almost no liquidity. The reasons for this are many, and most have already been hinted at. The company that issued the security is small, and most potential buyers of its securities will not have heard of it—so they have to do custom due diligence to be sure of what they are buying. Meanwhile, the seller has inside information that should be of concern to the buyer—why are they selling to me? And is this price a good one?

These securities are custom, so it is difficult for a buyer to be sure what they are buying without an in-depth and time-consuming process of discovery. The company may have rights to decide who can sell and who can buy their securities, and that process may be time-consuming and costly to the point that buyers may have left before companies approve a seller to sell. And so on.

Why Do We Do It This Way?

To summarize, early-stage technology company investing, as an example of a store of value, is a long way from being technology enabled as part of our digital revolution.

The securities being offered are custom, the process of selling them is in-person and often unrecorded, the cap table has not kept up with the technological innovations of our time, and the asset class is rife with inefficiencies, opaqueness, and lack of liquidity. It is also, perhaps, the highest returning asset class in the world today.

So why do we do it this way?

Because we have not got around yet to applying technology to this and other asset classes like small- and mid-capitalization real estate.

How It Might Work: Tokenization

For native digital assets to become a reality, we need a technology that allows for their creation and maintenance. While we will discuss this more fully in Part II of this book, we need to give the reader a peek into this topic so that you can understand the powerful innovation that tokenized assets would represent.

Digital assets can take the form of monies, commodities, collectibles, securities (equities or debt), revenue shares, profit participations, or any combination of these. The nature of the asset that results, and its codification into a form that can be easily issued, bought, and sold, is a significant challenge. Especially given the need for such assets to conform to current and future rules and regulations in a fully globalized internet that crosses all jurisdictions.

Such a complex undertaking is very hard to accomplish manually. Instead, software is being written that allows for the description of the asset, its terms and conditions, the rules by which it can be bought, held, and sold, and the laws that will apply to it, including the identities of those who will be allowed to participate in the market for it. The result of this work can be thought of as a "token" that describes everything mentioned above and which when held, provides the holder with its ownership and the full rights that this confers.

We will show later in the book that cryptocurrencies and cryptoassets are examples of tokens that have be created for specific purposes. There is now an emerging category of securitized tokens (STs), which are created to allow the partial ownership of some other asset to which they are secured. Early examples include the first tokenized venture fund, BCAP, offered by Blockchain Capital where Alison chairs the advisory board and that is issued now on the Securitize platform where Matthew is an advisory board member; Aspen digital where $18 million was raised by offering a fractional ownership of the St. Regis hotel in Aspen; the security token exchange being launched by Overstock and which raised

$134 million in equity with a revenue participation token deal; and even an example in which 31% of a work of art by Andy Warhol was offered as a fractional-ownership-asset-backed token raising $1.7 million.

Tokenization is the process by which assets will be made into these digital software tokens. The initial coin offering (ICO) proof of concept (POC) of 2017 and 2018 was an experiment in creating and selling tokens globally. We will return to the learnings of this POC later in the book.

What Do We Need Now?

Native digital assets for a fully digital world.

In this chapter, we have shown that it is not only the exchange of value that is rife with inefficiencies that are the legacy of our past. Some stores of value have also not yet felt the impact of technology enablement. Until they do, we are living in the middle of an unfinished digital revolution.

We opened this book by talking about how the search for competitive advantage in fast-changing spaces characterized by new innovations begins with the need to spot the "next big thing" and have a clear vision of what the future will look like. We contended that the next phase of the internet's evolution and the five big issues that will have to be resolved provide the matrix for the creation of powerful visions for projects and companies—they are the "next big thing" even if they are not singular in nature. They are the source of a great deal of value creation that will be unlocked over the next handful of decades. However, this is not only about economic gains.

If we succeed in solving these five main issues, as well as a host of smaller ones, society will gain all of the benefits of a digital future. If we fail, society may lose the benefits we have today as our internet becomes increasingly compromised and we drop back into a world before digitalization. Which some of us remember, but an increasingly large proportion of humanity has never experienced.

In order to take the next step in capturing competitive advantage in blockchain, you need to understand the new technologies and innovations that are likely to be enablers of your way to play. This is the focus of the next part of the book.

Part II | The Beauty of Blockchain

Chapter 7
The Story of Bitcoin and Why It Matters

It might make sense just to get some in case it catches on.
Once it gets bootstrapped, there are so many applications if
you could effortlessly pay a few cents to a website as easily as
dropping coins in a vending machine.

—Satoshi Nakamoto

In order to be able to leverage the power of new innovations and technologies to assist in creating value propositions and a way to play to meet the next big opportunities that we have outlined in Part I, we need to be clear about what these innovations and technologies are and how they may help us.

First we share the bitcoin story that drove a wave of new innovations and allowed the world to begin to see how our internet might be made much more powerful by them. Then in subsequent chapters we describe in turn the blockchain protocol, cryptoassets and tokenization, and the initial coin offering (ICO) proof of concept (POC).

A Compounding of Innovations

Importantly, this is not just a matter of blockchain and the innovations that it is making possible. This may also be about leveraging other emerging technologies and innovations into our way to play.

This transition towards a Fifth Era in which we are living is replete with new innovation upon new innovation, and as described in our executive summary, many of those innovations can be combined into powerful new ways of doing business. Artificial intelligence, the sensor revolution, distributed manufacturing, augmented reality, and so on, can all be combined with new approaches to, for example, digital payments and assets, to combine new value propositions.

However, in the context of this book, we will take as read that the central innovation around which we are building new value propositions—is that of the blockchain protocol and the consequent innovations of cryptoassets and new funding approaches, such as ICOs, that it has unleashed. Perhaps unfortunately, these innovations have been and continue to be confused with each other in the popular media. There are good reasons for this since they have been blended together in various combinations.

However, to get to grips with each and to know how to leverage them to create value propositions that address the big five issues that will be the world's focus, we need to unbundle them and discuss them each in turn. The best way to do this is to start with the initiative that started all of this—Satoshi Nakamoto's 2008 whitepaper on the formation of a new native digital money—bitcoin.

Bitcoin

We have already discussed in chapter 7 how the notion of native electronic monies is not a new one. We described experiments in the 1980s to create digital cash, and ever since innovators have put their minds to the problem of how to make this work in practice.

Other commentators have detailed those attempts, so we will not repeat them. However, suffice to say, it was not until 2008 and the launch of bitcoin, that the world first had a globally accepted native digital money that seemed to hold the potential to fulfill all three functions of money: unit of account, medium of exchange, and store of value.

The driving force for the creation of bitcoin appears to have been the global financial crisis that first hit in 2007 and extended through 2008. Economists see this as the most severe financial crisis that the world has experienced since the 1930s when the Great Depression destroyed the economies of many countries. This time the crisis was stimulated by the subprime mortgage market in the United States. The inability of the established financial system and the governments of the affected nations to stem the expansion of the crisis meant that it quickly rippled around the world taking down large financial institutions, such as Lehman Brothers, and driving the world into a deep economic downturn. This Great Recession in turn created enormous pressure, especially in Europe where the Euro and the countries using it suffered a banking system and debt crisis of enormous proportions.

It was against this backdrop that someone published a paper entitled "Bitcoin: A Peer-to-Peer Electronic Cash System" and shared open-source code for bitcoin software. Today the author remains anonymous other than the pen name "Satoshi Nakamoto," which appeared on the paper. By early 2009 (January 3, to be precise) the first block of the bitcoin blockchain was mined—this is known as the Genesis Block, and it includes the text: "The Times 03/Jan/2009 Chancellor on brink of second bailout for banks." By

2010 Nakamoto had mined one million bitcoins, which today would be worth over US $4 billion. Nakamoto then disappeared from the online bitcoin community, and we still do not know the author's identity or whether they, and their bitcoins, are still in existence.

Addressing the Internet's Shortcomings

The bitcoin white paper begins with an abstract that in its first few words calls out the importance of the innovations that will follow. We reproduce the first few words here:

> *Abstract: A purely peer-to-peer version of electronic cash would allow online payments to be sent directly from one party to another without going through a financial institution. Digital signatures provide part of the solution, but the main benefits are lost if a trusted third party is still required to prevent double-spending. We propose a solution to the double-spending problem using a peer-to-peer network. The network timestamps transactions by hashing them into an ongoing chain of hash-based proof-of-work, forming a record that cannot be changed without redoing the proof-of-work.* (2008)

In just these first few words, the author establishes that in order to create an effective e-cash they will address the issues of security and identity and trust, and do so in a way that also relies upon a distributed, decentralized network approach. In just a few words four of the five major issues confronting the internet are addressed.

By the end of the white paper, there is no question but that the fifth—native digital assets—can also be impacted with this new innovation. Indeed, today we can see that bitcoin itself probably serves as a better store of value than it satisfies the other two uses of money. However, other "bitcoins," or cryptoassets built on the blockchain protocol as laid out in the bitcoin whitepaper, are now focusing more on electronic assets than electronic cash, which was the purpose of Nakamoto's white paper.

Initial Bitcoin Adoption

The invention of bitcoin could have become an interesting but theoretical discussion between academics and scientists. However, after the 2008 great financial crisis driven by global demand for an e-cash free of government oversight and backing, bitcoin immediately found a worldwide user base.

As is so often the case with new technologies and innovations, the early users included those who live and work at the fringes of the organized economy. Very early on, bitcoin became the preferred money for illegal transactions undertaken in the dark web and on platforms such as Silk Road that were used for illegal commerce in drugs—among other goods. While bitcoin, with its immutable record of transactions held in public view, is actually a very insecure way to execute trades that the buyer and seller want to keep anonymous, at least for several years it became broadly accepted around the world for these purposes.

This initial use case afforded the opportunity for holders as well as new users to find additional purposes for the world's first widely used, distributed cryptocurrency. The first "legal" use cases involved remittances between parties who live in different countries that have reason to transact together but who want to avoid either the costs of traditional international monetary transfer methods, or for whatever reason, are usually disallowed from using them. Wences Casares, the Argentinean founder of Xapo—the bitcoin wallet and exchange—and a PayPal board director, puts it very succinctly when he says, "There are more people in the world who need a currency that they can trust than there are people in the world who can trust their currency." This is a profound point. While most observers in the organized developed markets scratched their heads at why they might need bitcoin, those hundreds of millions and billions of people in countries without reliable monies, or facing monetary controls that make it impossible to transact with friends and family or other parties in other countries, quickly saw in bitcoin a solution to their problems.

The number of holders of bitcoin and the number of transactions being undertaken began to increase rapidly in the period between 2012 and 2014. At this point, and combined with the realization that bitcoin's inbuilt long-term anti-inflation policies might combat value depreciation better than fiat currencies that can be printed at the whim of government backers, we saw the rise of a third and even more powerful use case—bitcoin as a store of value.

Bitcoin Today

Today bitcoin is a global money that continues to demonstrate utility against multiple use cases even though—or in some cases, because—there is no governmental agency standing behind it. The combined worldwide value of bitcoin at the time of writing is US $67 billion, at a price per bitcoin of around $3,800, and there are more miners and participants using the money than at any time to date—despite the volatility we have seen in the price of bitcoin. Compared to gold, bitcoin is just beginning to make a meaningful inroad into the store-of-value use case. However, as a fully technology-enabled native digital money and asset, bitcoin has paved a way to our future.

In summary, Nakamoto's 2008 bitcoin white paper and the sharing of the bitcoin software were enormously important because they, for the first time, demonstrated a way to implement a native digital money that anyone could use over the internet without needing to know the people with which they wished to transact. In order to do this, Nakamoto needed to create a new protocol that solved the issues of security and identity and trust that have been with the internet since inception. This new protocol, which solved these issues and yet did so in a way that was complementary to the communications protocols upon which the internet is based, is now called the blockchain protocol—the subject of the next chapter.

Chapter 8
The Blockchain Protocol

The interesting thing about blockchain is that it has made it possible for humanity to reach a consensus about a piece of data without having any authority to dictate it.

—Jaan Tallinn

In the previous chapter, we described the invention of bitcoin and the compounding of innovations that it represented. In order to continue to unbundle the parts, this chapter focuses on the first and most important innovation that the bitcoin whitepaper incorporated—that of the blockchain protocol.

What Are Blockchains?

Blockchains are open, distributed ledgers that can record transactions between two parties efficiently and in a verifiable and permanent way. They do this by building over time a chain of blocks of data, each of which records a set number of transactions that have occurred and each of which is "chained" both to the block that came before it and the block created after it. Hence, the name "blockchain."

Once written to the blockchain, each block cannot be modified without also changing the entire chain that follows it, which ensures its integrity. Each block is also stored on many computers in the network so that it can't be lost or destroyed. Each transaction in a block is timestamped and records the essentials of each transaction that has taken place including the parties, the nature of the transaction, and so on.

The blockchain and its constituent blocks can be examined by anyone in a fully public blockchain with cryptographic security designed in at the outset. One party to a transaction can, therefore, see the characteristics and behaviors of another party held in an immutable format. This makes the protocol ideal for use in a broadly distributed network in which many people participate, in which many transactions are taking place, and which over time many need to be revisited for whatever reason. As a result of these properties, blockchain holds the promise of being able to solve the first two big issues of security and identity and trust.

Other Benefits of Blockchain

Blockchains can also be made in a way that supports a distributed network of players and activities rather than requiring a central player to play a prominent role. While we have yet to understand how to make distributed networks occur for most human commercial transactions, it still provides the promise of solving the third big issue of an overly concentrating internet. This is part of the reason why there is so much excitement about the technology in those quarters where the redistribution of power and wealth are a primary objective.

There are other important characteristics of the first bitcoin blockchain that were also of vital significance in solving the native digital money issue. The blockchain only allows each bitcoin to be produced once—unlike most software that can be infinitely copied. It also allows for each bitcoin to be traced to who holds it today, and the provenance of who has ever held it since inception is also recorded and can be seen in plain view by examination of the blockchain. This means that it is very good at recording title rights. However, it is also very bad at maintaining anonymity. Indeed, law enforcement agencies have by this time learned to track down holders of bitcoin to their real identities when necessary to do so.

The technical description of how this works is not our interest, and so we will not go through topics such as hash, Merkle trees, consensus, and mining. All of these are very well described in other books by this time. Suffice to say that the blockchain protocol has revolutionized the thinking about how to take our communications internet and turn it into a commercial internet with native digital monies and assets. As Dan Morehead, founder and general partner of Pantera Capital explains, "We finally have a money over the internet protocol (MOIP) to complement all of the communications protocols upon which we depend."

Are All Blockchains Equal?

The bitcoin blockchain was the first, and it is supported by a ledger that is truly distributed, public, and immutable. However, each of those characteristics is a choice. Blockchain ledgers do not have to be fully distributed, public, or immutable. They can be centralized, private, and can include time-based truncation or archiving too. With each move away from the distributed, public, and immutable ledger characteristics, essential elements of the bitcoin blockchain are lost. However, for some purposes the trade-off may be worthwhile. The innovation implied by these new distributed ledgers is summarized in Sidebar 5.

Sidebar 5: Our World of Ledgers

Thousands of years ago humans began to trade together and with the invention of writing, began to make records of transactions between parties and the results of those transactions. Early moneylenders, for example, recorded what loans they made, on what date, to whom, and what amount of money was owed in return and by when.

These journals or ledgers were their stock-in-trade. Over time, the transaction history in those ledgers became valuable. It allowed them to assess what loans to make and what interest rates to charge. The moneylender was creating their own assessment of credit worthiness and the returns that they should charge should they decide to take the risk of lending again to those in their ledger.

Other moneylenders would find that information very valuable as they went about lending money themselves. This first moneylender could have chosen to share their ledger— to write its contents up on the wall of the temple for all to see. Humans could have begun with open, distributed ledgers.

However, we took a different road. Each ledger became the private personal property of its owner and was not shared. Rather, it became their source of competitive advantage. Because proprietary information is power.

Today, every human commercial transaction is recorded on ledgers, and almost all of them are private. Company books and accounting ledgers. Banking ledgers. Registries of assets and their ownership. Lists of who works where and what they are paid. The list is endless.

Our world is almost 100% running on private, centralized ledgers.

It is a very big concept to think that with technology we might now enter a world of open, distributed ledgers. Everything that we think is the right way to do commerce just might be about to change.

While blockchains are not the only way to support the creation of digital monies or digital assets (you can use conventional technology solutions too), readers should not be confused by the back and forth of traders, some of whom are long and some short on cryptoassets and so write pro or cons in their posts and blogs. Look instead to how the major financial institutions are acting to see what is really happening. It is not without import that major players like Fidelity, Goldman Sachs, and JPMorgan Chase are choosing to launch their own solutions based upon the blockchain protocol even if they may be leaning towards proprietary private options at this time.

In summary, the blockchain protocol that was embedded into the bitcoin whitepaper was transformative since it defined an approach for creating distributed ledgers that are open and immutable, which in turn addresses the issues of security and identity and trust that are central to the internet's continued evolution. Bitcoin's blockchain does this in a decentralized, distributed fashion that provides a blueprint to combat the third issue of excessive centralization and control. In the next chapter, we turn to the issue of how cryptoassets including cryptocurrencies can be built on a platform that leverages a version of the blockchain protocol.

Chapter 9
Cryptoassets and Tokens

It's inevitable that security tokens will transform equity just as bitcoin has transformed currency, because they afford the owner a direct, liquid economic interest and the expedited delivery of proceeds. Every type of ownership can be tokenized, which is a massive multi-trillion dollar addressable market.

—Carlos Domingo

The second innovation that is available for leveraging into a way to play strategy is the cryptoasset and tokenization innovation. This is particularly important to understand because at the end of the day any new digital money or asset will likely need to leverage this emerging body of innovation and technology.

What Are Cryptoassets?

Bitcoin is a cryptocurrency in that it is a digital, computer-based money that can be used to make monetary transactions between parties. It can also be a store of value, and there is some evidence that in the specific case of bitcoin, more people decide to hold it than to trade it. So it is actually a better store of value than it is a means of payment. Other early cryptocurrencies are not all equally opaque to external scrutiny as allowed for by the bitcoin block-chain. Zcash and Monero are examples that provide for a great deal of anonymity in the way they are designed.

The value of any given cryptocurrency depends upon the balance of supply and demand. On the supply side, some like bitcoin have limited supply built into their design. However, others do not. What this means is that buyers need to understand what the nature of each cryptocurrency is and what the likely future supply will be. The demand is of course much less easy to quantify, and there are probably already far more candidates for becoming global digital monies than there are likely to be winners.

These new monies are also used in the creation of networks of supporters who are being incentivized to work with and for the protocol or project of which the money is a part. So, for example, new crypto tokens may be issued to miners who are doing the computing work, developers who are writing code to expand the functionality of the protocol, or users who are referring, using, and promoting the protocol and its applications. This is very powerful. Communities can be incentivized by their own home-grown monies just as videogames use virtual currencies within their digital worlds.

Bitcoin and all other cryptocurrencies are also software, and each one's specific characteristics were decided by the computer scientist that designed it—Satoshi Nakamoto in the case of bitcoin. Nakamoto could have chosen to design bitcoin to be a store of value but not a payment method. In which case we would say that it is a cryptoasset but not a cryptocurrency.

This is more than a question of pedantry. Cryptoassets built upon their own blockchains can be designed by their computer scientist to accomplish almost any task that creativity can put a blockchain to. So for the balance of this book we will use the broader cryptoasset nomenclature.

Cryptoassets are digital "tokens" that are linked to blockchains and which have the ability to perform certain purposes that their makers have designed into them.

How to Classify Cryptoassets?

We are already seeing great creativity being exerted by computer scientists who have been able to create thousands of cryptoassets. In order to get to grips with their variety of use cases, Richard Muirhead and Max Mersch of Fabric Ventures in London have come up with a taxonomy that we find helpful. There are three main types of cryptoassets:

- **Currencies and Commodities**—these are focused on enabling payments and stores of value within our digital economy and can be further divided into three types: store of value tokens, stablecoins, and payment tokens.
- **Utility Tokens**—these focus on providing incentives in the context of digital communities that may be creating networks of common interest to accomplish given tasks. They can be further divided into governance tokens, discount tokens, work tokens, including pure work, curated registries, access-based tokens, and burn and mint tokens.
- **Security Tokens**—these are tokens that represent the value of an underlying asset. These can be divided into many types, but examples include equity-backed tokens, bond- or note-backed tokens, real-estate-backed tokens,

revenue-backed tokens, fine-art- or collectible-backed tokens, fund tokens, and so on.

This is a work in process only limited by the imagination of the computer scientists that are coming up with new token attributes that might allow them to fulfill valuable use cases.

How many of these use cases will prove valuable in the real world and how many specific cryptoassets are needed in each case will be seen in time. The team at Fabric currently believes there will only be a few successful currency and commodity tokens with global usage of which bitcoin, Ethereum, Zcash, Monero, and some stablecoins are considered to be outstanding candidates

However, while there may be many more utility tokens and security tokens, their respective use cases are likely to be more limited in scope. For example, a recent security token tied to the St. Regis hotel in Aspen, Colorado, is only going to have utility for a handful of investors who chose to invest in it.

When Is a Token a Utility or a Security?

The first wave of token offerings was for what were described as "utility" tokens. This created some consternation among investors and regulators—especially those in the US—because the offerings seemed in many cases to be for investment opportunities but were lacking in the discipline that is required of offerings to investors. Many appeared to be breaking even the most basic rules of engagement.

In the US, this came to a head when the SEC concluded in July 2018 that the DAO token offering on the Ethereum platform was subject to federal securities law and that the token offered was a security, not a utility. This had serious implications since the DAO offering, as had been the case in many others too, had not met the basic rules expected by the SEC for offerings under their management. At the same time, the SEC also provided guidance that Ether, the token of the Ethereum protocol itself, was indeed a utility token as it was being used to power a broadly distributed operating system without any promise of future investment returns.

These two landmark decisions coming at the same time created great consternation, especially over the definition of "utility" versus "security"—not least because of the very significant differences in treatment that would result.

So how do we determine whether something is one or the other? The starting point is to see if the token is primarily functioning as a way to power a distributed network without any expectation of an increase in value. If so, it will have an active role in motivating or incentivizing the development of the code, in incentivizing community participation in some way, including in processing and validating transactions on the protocol, or it will be clearly serving some similar purpose today. The network itself will be clearly distributed without any narrowly defining interests in control or the prospect of seeing substantial personal gains, and no one will be buying the token as a way to make money through ownership of a financial trading or storage instrument. If the token meets all of these characteristics, it may have some prospect of being classified as a utility or perhaps a commodity token. At this point, it might make sense to get a legal opinion—but few tokens do meet all of these criteria.

Conversely, security tokens are intended to be financial instruments that will provide future profits and/or gain, and investors are buying them for that purpose. While security tokens may come in various forms—equity-backed, bond-backed, fund-backed, real-estate-backed, commodity-backed, revenue- or royalty-backed, and so on—they all share this central characteristic: investors are buying them for the expectation of making money. All tokens that meet these criteria are automatically securities and so are currently subject to securities regulation and policy. While we may one day see newly tailored securities laws for these types of innovative and creative securities, today they are covered by the existing body of legislation depending upon the jurisdiction of issuer, buyer, and sometimes intermediary.

This is a light sketch of what is actually a very complex painting, and none of our readers should rely upon these words to make important decisions regarding their tokens and how to classify them. They need to get expert advice.

Just as importantly, investors need to conduct their own due diligence and know for sure what they are buying if they do decide to acquire any token of any type. For the most part, in 2017 and 2018, the issuers of tokens have been sloppy and often have been so in order to take advantage of their backers and investors. We are very happy to see the marketplace becoming more disciplined and the mass of badly defined or presented offerings being flushed away in favor of those with great teams, well-constructed plans, and keen appreciation for the purpose they serve today and in the future. These are the offerings that deserve to find backers.

Sidebar 6 details how Securitize is building out a global

compliance layer for digital asset creation that directly addresses this challenge.

Sidebar 6: Securitize

As we have noted, the challenges of ensuring compliance in offerings being made across global jurisdictions is immense. The ICO boom and bust demonstrated just how easy it is to break rules in one place when issuing tokens from another. However, without solutions that ensure that the offerings are meeting the requirements of local regulators, the promise of technology-enabled investing cannot be reached.

One new company seeking to meet this challenge is Securitize whose platform is designed to solve this challenge.

- **End-to-End Platform**—Securitize is a full-stack technology and services platform with powerful features and specialized tools for both investors and issuers. The Securitize platform allows users to manage their digital securities from one convenient dashboard.
- **Coded Compliance**—Securitize's digital securities (DS) protocol provides a complete, flexible, and adopted compliance solution in the market today. The DS protocol ensures digital securities issued via the Securitize platform can be traded compliantly across all marketplaces and exchanges.

> • **Open Platform**—the open platform enables Securitize to focus on primary issuance and lifecycle management while leveraging partner network and driving protocol adoption. By listening to their customers and counsel Securitize better facilitates the compliant issuance and trading of digital securities on a global scale.

Securitize's digital securities (DS) protocol has the highest adoption rate in the market today and provides a seamless compliant integration solution for issuers, investors, and exchanges throughout the entire digital security lifecycle—from initial issuance, to trading, distribution, and governance.

Source: Securitize white paper and websites.

Key Requirements for Tokenization

In order for native digital assets (tokenized assets) to succeed, they need to meet the key requirements of the various players who come together to buy and sell those assets. In its simplest form we have four key constituents in most asset markets.

One—Issuers

First we have those who own or create an asset that they would then like to sell to other people.

For issuers their key requirements are the following: that they have secure and trusted ways to register their asset (digital registries) and attach it to a digital format so that others will trust in it; that they gain access to primary issuance approaches that will enable them to reach enough people with capital; and that they land secondary market solutions that will allow for the ongoing support of the marketplace and secondary trading of the asset in ways that encourage primary purchasing.

Two—Investors

On the other side of each transaction, the investors need a number of things to be willing to buy issuer securities. Aside from the obvious requirements of a good asset, which has been subject to deep and independent due diligence, and which is being sold at a good price, investors want access to high-quality deal flow, easy-to-use investment platforms, and future liquidity for their investments in the form of secondary markets that will allow them to sell on their investments, should they want to do so. They also need high-quality ways to track and assess their investment portfolios.

Three—Intermediaries—Exchanges and Distributors

Between buyers and sellers sit the intermediaries who facilitate the effective operation of a marketplace. These include exchanges, distributors of all sorts, and in the case of digital assets, new players such as digital wallet providers and custodians.

These intermediaries want to see high-quality deal flow from issuers. They need easy on- and off-ramps on either side of their activities so that they can easily get assets on to their platform from issuers and easily pass them on to investors if the investors prefer to hold them with other players. And they need seamless syndication solutions that allow assets to be bought and sold from other intermediaries to meet the needs of investors on the platform.

Four—Governments/Regulators

Traded asset marketplaces are almost always tightly controlled to ensure that bad actors and bad practices cannot surface. In most cases governments establish regulations and bodies to enforce them. Those regulatory bodies' key requirements include adherence to the laws, ongoing transparency so that this adherence can be tracked and assured, and filters that actively surface and call out bad actors and practices. For the first time, the prospect of real-time transparency appears possible as noted by Jamie Finn, co-founder of Securitize, who put it this way, "The accelerating trend of tokenization of securities along with blockchain's ability to enable trustless triple-entry accounting will provide what shareholders and regulators have always wanted: true transparency with instant execution."

Sidebar 7 provides an example of a new-world platform that is being built to support both traditional and tokenized asset investment and trading approaches.

Sidebar 7: Linqto

With the prospect of a world of tokenized assets comes the prospect that investors will see the elimination of many of the challenges that they confront today in private investing. Unlike the public markets for equity and debt, the private markets are still reliant upon paper-based processes that are time-consuming, costly, and complex. This in turn makes it hard for issuers to tap into global investor communities; it makes it unattractive for many investors to participate; and

---

it limits the ability to make secondary markets for the private assets. Without secondary markets there is no liquidity, which in turn again makes the assets less attractive to investors.

Linqto is an example of a fully integrated private investment platform that plans to not only support the buying and trading of traditional private equity investments—from company equity and debt, to real estate and other asset classes—but will also allow for blockchain-based digital registries and eventually tokenized assets.

Linqto's acquisition of PrimaryMarkets in 2018 brought a functioning digital registry and trading platform into the solution. Linqto has now partnered with globaliD to enable seamless know-your-client (KYC)/anti-money laundering (AML) work to be done. Linqto has also partnered with Securitize to build out the digital registry and tokenization solutions.

Carlos Domingo, co-founder of Securitize, emphasizes the potential impact of the arrival of native digital assets. As he explains, "Tokenizing real-world assets is probably the most disruptive trend as we digitize trillions of dollars of our financial system using blockchain technologies and the distributed ledger to record ownership and facilitate transactions. What bitcoin did to money, blockchain technology will do to the concept of ownership. New ways of owning assets will emerge that we cannot possibly imagine today."

In the next chapter, we review the third innovation that quickly took off after the launch of bitcoin—a wave of initial coin offerings (ICOs) that were used to broadly distribute thousands of new cryptoassets that were built on versions of the blockchain protocol, including Ethereum. This powerful new approach to capital formation may be the harbinger of new ways of conducting financial investments and managing markets and liquidity.

Chapter 10
Initial Coin Offerings (ICOs)

The crypto market has set the bar shockingly low for entrepreneurs to raise money, and this is dangerous for everyone involved.

—Nick Tomaino

We now come to the third innovation that has also become by far the most controversial: the initial coin offering (ICO).

What Are ICOs?

Readers have many ways to raise capital for their projects and businesses, and a technology-enabled approach is by no means required. However, anyone contemplating launching new business models—specifically those aiming to create communities that collaborate and create value together on a platform; or those solving the digital monies or assets challenges—should be fully conversant with the ICO innovation too, at a minimum, because it provides glimpses into the future that you are trying to make happen.

An ICO is the event during which a new cryptoasset or token is offered to the public or members of a targeted community, either in a fully open process or in a private placement. We have already discussed in the prior chapter just why new blockchain communities are being supported by cryptoassets, which are used to incentivize the participants and make them active members of the network. In this context, ICOs can be thought of as a version of technology-enabled crowdfunding. In this sense they do represent the future—utilizing technology to allow primary issuance of new assets to occur on a global basis without the complexity, cost, and delays that paper-based processes inevitably generate. During 2017 and 2018 we saw a global proof of concept (POC) as the world, for a short time, embraced the ICO phenomenon. However, this POC of the feasibility of technology-enabled private investing was not without significant challenges.

First Proof of Concept (POC)

The earliest ICO was held by Mastercoin in the summer of 2013, with Ethereum launching its ICO in 2014. Prior to this, cryptoassets had been distributed in other ways—in the case of bitcoin, it was necessary to do computing work in order to earn bitcoins (mining). By 2017 there was an explosion of ICOs with more than US $8 billion being raised in the first half of 2018 alone, and perhaps US $20 billion between mid-2017 and mid-2018.

Despite these early pilots, the global POC for offering cryptoassets to global investors through a technology-enabled crowdfunding process was the recent 2017 and 2018 ICO boom and bust. During this period, several thousand new technology projects created tokens, which were sold to investors who were often, but not always, members of the community or network supporting the project. Perhaps as much as US $20 billion at then values was invested although no authoritative source has tracked all offers and all capital invested.

Many different claims were made for the utility of these projects and for the outcomes that they would be able to achieve. Without question, bad actors followed bad practices to take advantage of this new way of raising capital. Many of those fake projects have since vaporized. Meanwhile, in the stark light of day, many others have been shown to be overly optimistic, poorly thought through, badly presented, illegal, and sometimes all four.

Broken Laws and Adverse Selection

By mid-2018 the major regulators in jurisdictions, such as China, Korea, Japan, the UK, and the US, began to clamp down on ICOs for a number of reasons. First and foremost, they judged that the majority of the offerings were not utility tokens as had been claimed by their issuers but rather security tokens. Security tokens, like all securities, are covered by specific legislation, and in most cases that legislation had been ignored during the POC.

Of even more serious concern were the widespread Ponzi schemes, scams, and fraudulent behavior that surfaced during these months. Simply put, many of the ICOs were not real. Fake teams, fake projects, unrealistic expectations for what could be delivered, misleading "guarantees" of the returns that would come from buying tokens—the list was long. It appears that as many as 50% of the offerings were not well founded, and of the ICOs that occurred in the second half of 2017, almost half had already failed or been abandoned by February 2018. Sidebar 8 explains how a few of the ICO scams worked as a cautionary note to readers who might be considering diving in next time around.

Sidebar 8: ICO Scams

Throughout history there have been creative swindlers who have put together schemes to defraud people out of their money. This is nothing new. However, with the creation of technology-enabled investing approaches, the potential scope and scale of these scams can become enormous. Without trying to be comprehensive, this sidebar details four examples of common scams so that readers can be the wiser as they consider future opportunities.

- **Create Projects You Never Plan to Complete**—the simplest scam of all is to raise money into a project that is never intended to become a real initiative. During 2017 and 2018 there were hundreds of such scams perpetrated on unsuspecting and somewhat naive investors. Experienced investors conduct detailed due diligence specifically to weed out these sorts of situations. However, in many cases ICO investors conducted no due diligence. An example here is Shenzhen Puyin Blockchain, a Chinese issuer that raised over US $60 million through the projects ACChain, Puyin Blockchain, and BioLifeChain. None of these proved to be real, and the Chinese police have, to date, made six arrests.
- **Write Fake Project White Papers**—taking the scam one a step further, issuers sometimes created altogether fake write-ups of their projects—plagiarizing

other people's work and/or creating fake profiles of teams sometimes using third-party identities without even letting the people know that their likenesses were now team members in an ICO offering. An example of this approach is Block Broker, which, ironically, promised to eliminate ICO fraud by building a safe investment platform. Block Broker was highly rated by ICO agencies and raised over US $3 million before it turned out that the image of the CEO in the white paper was actually of a photographer who had nothing to do with the project. While any due diligence process would have uncovered this scam earlier, in this case the ICO investors clearly did not meet the team perpetrating the fraud.

- **Conduct Pump and Dumps**—these are nothing new in the world of investing. Issuers and sometimes "pump-and-dump groups" work to convince others to buy the stock, thus increasing the price in the process. When the price has risen sufficiently, the issuer and/or pump-and-dump group sells their own stock leaving the new investors holding the baby, which may be a real but overvalued project or may actually be an example of scam one or two. In the world of online social sites and digital exchanges and trading, pump and dumps have become highly sophisticated, with large groups of thousands of online investors working together to drive up the prices of a cryptoasset before rapidly dumping it.

The process is not without its risks for the pump and dumpers too since often not moving fast enough can leave a pump and dumper also facing a greatly depreciated asset that is hard to sell.

- **Build Ponzi Schemes**—scams are not only online. There have been good examples of hardware-based Ponzi schemes created in the new world of mining hardware sold to support blockchain communities. It works like this: a scammer sets up as a "sponsor" to sell server hardware configured for mining a specific cryptoasset to unwitting investors with the promise that they will make high returns. For example, if they buy a server for, say, US $1,000, they then receive back, say, US $100, from the sponsor in each of the first few weeks of operation. Meanwhile, the sponsor asks them to encourage their own friends to also buy the package since the returns are clearly impressive and assured. The sponsor then takes the money from the latest buyers of the equipment and uses it to show returns to the earlier buyers. This may continue through several rounds by which time the Ponzi pyramid will have grown greatly and the next wave of buyers may be investing many millions into the scheme. At that time, the Ponzi perpetrator simply disappears as do the fake investment returns from the mining equipment. Filecoin has been an example of a cryptoasset being used by third-party hardware Ponzi schemes in China, and the challenge of closing them down is significant for the US-based Filecoin team.

These are just examples that are mostly retail-investor-facing while much larger-in-scale exchange scams, such as painting the tape and exchange price manipulation, have been widespread too. The creativity with which scammers have used schemes from the world of traditional investing and ported them over to the ICO world has been amazing, not only for their brazenness and for the scale with which they have been able to ramp the scams up, but also for the naivety with which they have been received by ICO investors who have been willing to invest their money without even perfunctory due diligence.

Positive Learnings

Even with all of the legal issues, bad actors, and bad behaviors, this 18-month POC offered a number of powerful insights and demonstrated clear benefits that future native digital assets efforts might provide. The benefits that the ICO POC demonstrated include these:

- Ability to attach complex investor rights into smart contract tokens
- Feasibility of recording tokens on digital registers with immutable record of change of ownerships and transparency (blockchain-based digital registers)

- Lower friction and transaction costs where digital assets are offered to online investors
- Ability to facilitate access to global investors including those unknown to typical issuers
- Ability to use technology to greatly factionalize ownership into small lot sizes while still ensuring economic viability
- Increased market depth and liquidity due to both the global reach of the offerings and the high demand for many of the leading projects
- This is a partial list but already an impressive one for a POC that only lasted for a few months.

A Host of Concerns

The other side of the ICO POC coin was of course that many mistakes were made and the need for new policies, procedures, and approaches became apparent. These represent barriers to the implementation of new and better native digital asset solutions. Principal in overcoming these barriers are the following:

- More education of investors so that they are better able to discriminate between good and bad projects given the new, complex, and challenging technologies being represented by project teams, many of whom do not have experience with these technologies or in bringing other technologies to market
- Better ways to assess due diligence issuers to ensure that bad actors are filtered out at the outset
- Need for clear guidance from regulators in all jurisdictions

that will have an impact on how they expect native digital assets to be offered, held, and eventually sold

- Creation of new technologies that allow these policies to be put into place and their enforcement to be transparent to those tasked with ensuring adherence
- Better or more marketplaces that are able to provide both primary issuance and ongoing secondary trading in reliable and secure ways
- More compliant platforms that ensure that new digital assets are able to be created in compliant ways and that have the inbuilt intelligence to ensure that they remain compliant as they are traded on into the future
- Common standards to allow syndication between intermediaries and common understanding between issuers and investors

No doubt there are other important ways to overcome barriers to adoption, but this list provides substantial work for the immediate future. Of critical importance to all of this is the challenge of making a new invention, cryptoassets, fit the existing regulatory frameworks that are in place for conducting asset purchase, sales, and storage.

As US Commodities Futures Trading Commission chairman J. Christopher Giancarlo recently said, "We are entering a new digital era in world financial markets. As we saw with the development of the internet, we cannot put the technology genie back in the bottle. Virtual currencies mark a paradigm shift in how we think about payments, traditional financial processes, and engaging in economic activity. Ignoring these developments will not make them go away, nor is it a responsible regulatory response."

In conclusion, Satoshi Nakamoto's 2008 bitcoin white paper ushered in three principal innovations that have already begun to make real the promise of native digital monies and digital assets. The blockchain protocol, cryptoassets and tokens, and ICOs are all important innovations and forerunners of a new world that we are beginning to understand. Taken together, they offer the prospect of a digital world that takes the internet we already have—complements it and redesigns it to include the blockchain protocol—and uses the combination to solve the primary issues of security, identity and trust, concentration, and native digital monies and assets. For readers seeking to build a way to play and a right to win, these technologies are important and may be instrumental.

In the next chapter, we explore some broader uses of blockchain technology that established corporations are exploring—beyond the three functions of money: unit of account, medium of exchange, and store of value. The ensuing chapter's examples are indications of how established companies are seeking new ways to play and are attempting to make themselves more capable competitors by leveraging the blockchain innovation. These examples may provide seeds of ideas for your own way to play while also illustrating that blockchain is not only the domain of new project teams and early-stage startups.

Chapter 11
Corporate Applications of Blockchain

The Americans have need of the telephone, but we do not. We have plenty of messenger boys.

—William Preece, British Post Office

It's just not a real thing, eventually it [bitcoin] will be closed.

—Jamie Dimon, JPMorgan Chase

While we have emphasized digital monies and digital payments as the more important issues to address as we move the internet forward, established companies have a host of other business challenges that need to be addressed and which incorporate aspects of security and identity and trust. In a world that will increasingly be connected and reliant upon fully digital approaches, the current technology infrastructure is beginning to creak at the seams. Consequently large established businesses are exploring the blockchain protocol to see how it might transform existing business processes—from registries and record-keeping, to supply chain management, to better data collection, analysis, and sharing, and more. In some cases this is work to support broader strategies; in others it is the driver of new ways of competing. This chapter summarizes how established companies are exploring new ways to capture competitive advantage with the blockchain innovation.

What Happened Last Time Around

It took the world a long time to realize what TCP/IP and the internet meant for our way of life. The initial innovations of the 1970s and 1980s were still only used by a handful of scientists and academics as we entered the 1990s—to share information—mostly text-based. During these decades, larger companies were confused and often paralyzed by indecision concerning what to do about the internet. Some tried pilots, some began to get traction, but most sat on the sidelines. In retrospect the large companies that did the best were at least fast followers—although being a pioneer also brings substantial risk of failure, which a fast follower can often avoid.

What key lessons does the corporate adoption of the internet provide us that might help set strategy for the next great protocol—blockchain?

In the late-1980s, a few pioneering people began to apply the communications protocols, and the internet platform built upon it to more powerful purposes than sending academic messages and information. The first handful of ecommerce websites began to be developed, and the first handful of users began to visit them and even make purchases.

We were consultants at consulting firms McKinsey and AT Kearney during this period, and began to be asked to help larger companies apply this technology to their own businesses. In the early 1990s we worked on an effort at Sears that included assessing the prospects and potential value of that retailer's online internet service provider (ISP) Prodigy. The insights that project provided proved valuable as we invested in Catalina Marketing and AOL, and rode their ascent for most of the 1990s. After next leading a smatter of similar projects, we worked with Dave Coulter, CEO of Bank of America, and his online leaders, Mike DeVico and George Cheng, as they successfully launched BankAmerica.com and the bank's online payment businesses. Soon Bank of America was one of the world's leading online banks, and customers were visiting the website constantly to check balances, make simple transfers, and explore the bank's offerings.

Matthew's leaving consulting to be head of strategy and corporate development for Gap, just as physical goods retailers began to go online, was equally exciting and also confusing. Gap in quick succession launched BananaRepublic.com, Gap.com, and then OldNavy.com. In every case naysayers and cynics threw cold water as well as very legitimate criticisms at the initiatives. Would customers want this? Could you buy clothing without feeling it and trying it on? Would price transparency collapse the pricing structure of lines? Would we end up with channel and brand conflict and cannibalization? How would customers cope when they bought something online and tried to change sizes in store only to discover that their product was online only? And a host of other fears and threats. As head of strategy we needed answers, but no one had them. Even then most creative minds struggled to see how Amazon could stretch beyond book sales, and other leading retailers in other categories waited to see what all this meant.

Then, like a rising tide, the POCs turned into viable businesses, which excited and then amazed customers. As word of mouth spread the story, more and more people went online for the first time, clicked on a book to buy, and then laughed out loud when Amazon seemed to read their minds in coming back with suggestions for what to buy next.

Matthew's personal moment of clarity came in about 1996. Preparing to interview for a chief-of-marketing job at a leading brand company, he went to the expert on branding at AT Kearney and asked for a book that he might read that would give him a better sense of what the latest thinking was on driving brand equity. He went to Amazon and bought the book, read it quickly, and then went back to the expert for more recommendations. She gave him three more titles. Back to Amazon, back to his account, and there, in plain view, Amazon was suggesting five books of which three were the same ones that the AT Kearney expert had just suggested minutes ago. How could Amazon know more than one of the world's leading marketing experts? Furthermore, Amazon could do this across every single area of human knowledge.

Alison shortly after joined Barclays Global Investors (BGI) as CFO and head of strategy, and there too the internet was shaking up everyone. BGI was already the world's largest asset manager with trillions of dollars under management, and the exchange-traded funds (ETF) business was just beginning to take off. However, the question was just being asked whether BGI could and should provide its ETF products to retail consumers as well as institutional customers. The internet raised the prospect of broad distribution for new and innovative financial products, and players, from Schwab, to Ameritrade, to Bank of America, were beginning to stretch the limits of online offerings. For BGI this became a new initiative—iShares—which is today a multi-trillion-dollar asset business within Blackrock, which acquired BGI from Barclays in 2007.

These are just a handful of examples of a tidal wave of adoption that swept every industry, every product, and every service into our current digital economy. The internet has impacted everything humans do. Today we look back and can't imagine that so many people doubted so vehemently its eventual efficacy. Even one of its leading architects Robert Metcalfe, who by then was the founder of 3Com, said, "The internet will soon go spectacularly supernova and in 1996 catastrophically collapse." His timing was way off, but unless we solve the five big issues of security, identity and trust, concentration, native digital monies, and native digital assets, his prediction may still yet come to pass.

Keys Lessons Learned

These are the key lessons learned from these direct experiences and observations:

- A lot of money was lost by those corporations that dove in first, without a clearly defined understanding of what this all meant for their core businesses. Being at the "bleeding edge" provided insights but was expensive.
- Conversely, it was important to be around the new innovation—observing, learning, building relationships, and gaining access—so that when things became real, it would be possible to move fast.
- Watching how end users were adopting the new

technologies, even in industries that might not seem directly relevant, gave great insights into the eventual course of adoption and change in a person's own industry. Those who did best during the rollout of the internet understood the types of value that could be delivered to their customers ahead of their competitors.

- The learning from the prior point was the importance of watching competitors very closely—including those that may seem to be too early on the scene, "flailing about," wasting money and resources. The reason it was important is that the glimmers of what would prove to be the "killer apps" in each industry were beginning to become apparent in those early competitor experiments.

- A similar strategy that many corporations put to good effect was to get close to the leading disruptor companies early. As the inevitable shakeout occurred in each group of industry disruptors, a handful became attractive acquisition candidates. Only a few players in most industries were able to lock in, usually through acquisitions, these winners. That was often a source of competitive advantage.

This provides some context for what we are beginning to see happen in blockchain as regards corporate engagement. We will revisit this topic in more detail in the chapter on corporate competitive advantage in blockchain later in this book.

Everyone Working On It

Where do we stand with respect to the development of the block-chain protocol and the software stack being built on top of it at the time of the writing of this book? Jalak Jobanputra, founder and general partner of Future\Perfect Ventures, explains, "Blockchain technology is in nascent stages and in the long run undoubtedly has the potential to change the way we interact with each other as well as how enterprises conduct business. As an investor, it's important to understand that people and corporations take time to adapt to new technologies and new behaviors—it is not an overnight or one-year process."

Today large companies in every industry are launching POCs and partnering with innovative teams and projects to explore the application of blockchain to their businesses just as was the case in the early 1990s as ecommerce first took off. Outlier is a corporate research service that tracks these POCs. In early 2019 Outlier is tracking 293 blockchain initiatives at major corporations across every industry and in almost every country. Some of their insights include:

- The majority of blockchain POCs are in financial services with some 55% share across all sectors from capital markets and banking to insurance where the focus is on the three functions of money.
- The second largest engagement is in the technology sector specifically across all sectors of ecommerce where the focus is on uses beyond the functions of money. These include registries and applications that allow multiple

players across an integrated process to collaborate more effectively—especially along the supply chain.

- Every industry has ongoing work exploring the protocol's applications.
- The US leads with 25% of the POCs, followed by China (14%), Japan (13%), UAE (6%), the UK (5%), and then a long tail of nations including all of the largest by GDP measures.

Outlier also details the explosion of patent activity in the space, which is itself a reflection of the seriousness with which corporate research and development centers are taking this new innovation. These include leaders such as Amazon, Boeing, IBM, and Western Union. Of course patents will limit the ability of a distributed community to further innovate, so this is a double-edged sword.

Industry Examples

Without attempting to be comprehensive, the following are examples in some of the world's largest industries:

Aviation

IBM has created a consortium on its Hyperledger platform to examine the use case for blockchain along the industry's supply chain, and leading airlines and aircraft original equipment manufacturers (OEMs) are collaborating on its development. Air France, Boeing, and Lufthansa have been particularly vocal on their development efforts.

Automobiles

The global automotive industry sees many innovations that are already impacting its business including artificial intelligence, autonomous vehicles, connected control systems, electric vehicles, ride sharing, and others. Many of these innovations require micro-transactions to succeed, and conventional payment mechanisms are not able to cost effectively support this today. As a result, blockchain holds out the promise of creating a solution that would work well for the internet of things including in the automotive sector. All of the automotive leaders are working on these matters including BMW, Daimler, Toyota, and Volkswagen.

Financial Services

Banks, including American Express, BNY Mellon, Citibank, Goldman Sachs, Mastercard, Santander, RBC, JPMorgan, and Visa, among others, are all investing in blockchain POCs across many areas of their business and in some cases have set up fulltime teams to work on them.

There is a keen appreciation across the financial services world that the legacy systems upon which trading takes place are in need of overhaul and that a new technology that can change the fundamentals of how players interact with each other in market-places could be transformative. As Bill Sarris, co-founder and CTO of Linqto, explains, "The only difference in private market trading versus public market trading is the friction between bid and settlement. Blockchain will reduce that friction to 'tZero.' By 2021, we will be trading private equity, cryptocurrencies, and equity in real estate as easily as trading stocks on the NASDAQ today."

Fine Art and Collectibles

Fine art and collectibles are much less valuable when their history is unclear, and much of the work and cost of the industry goes into trying to backtrack each time an item comes up for auction to see if a clear provenance can be created.

A consortium of the leading auction software providers have backed Codex as a blockchain-based solution to this problem. Other initiatives are also underway, including initiatives throughout the market for high-value products traded at auction rather than through conventional retailers.

Healthcare

The questions of security and validated identity and information management are very important in the healthcare industry and very challenging given the fragmentation and reliance on legacy processes and infrastructure. Therefore, major areas of development in healthcare include these:

- **Medical Records**—an industry blockchain might provide an immutable medical record for any individual. This could remove both the errors and the risks medical records create for patients and practitioners.
- **Consent Management**—an industry blockchain solution might then be combined with patient consent purposes so that each patient can control their own data and decide what access to provide each potential user—whether practitioner, provider, or payee.
- **Supply Chain Management**—the healthcare industry has

one of the most complex and largest supply chain systems in which accuracy, security, and integrity are critical. As a result, players, such as IBM, are trying to facilitate the creation of industry supply chain consortiums.

In pharmaceuticals and medical devices, blockchain is being explored as a source of micropayments, registers, and collaboration solutions.

Publishing

Publishing is an interesting case study. Perhaps more than any other industry, media was dramatically impacted by the arrival of the internet. Today whether publishers focus on books, film, music, news, television, or some other area of content, there are no publishers who have not begun to think about how to avoid a second disruption to their business that might be forthcoming with the arrival of blockchain.

Alex Fedosseev of 1World Online, which serves traditional news publishers globally, puts it this way, "All publishers are keen on engaging and retaining their audiences, especially since they have, in many cases, seen them draining away to social media and news aggregators. So incentives and loyalty programs, based on blockchain, like 1World tokens, are helping them solve this existential problem."

Retailing

In retailing, knowing the provenance and quality of products is a critical and complex undertaking. On the one hand, fakes, stolen goods, and pirated goods are everywhere. On the other, when goods go bad and customers suffer, governments expect the retailers and their suppliers to be able to move quickly to solve the issue.

Examples of use cases being pursued include De Beers backing the use of blockchain to track diamonds, with the creation of Everledger and Cedex as examples of private startups solving pieces of this challenge. At the other end of the spectrum, Wal-Mart has been deploying blockchain to track leafy products (cabbage, lettuce, spinach, etc.) from source to store not least because of the recent and catastrophic recalls of such products as a result of E. coli outbreaks.

Shipping

The global shipping industry is huge and very backward in terms of its practices along its supply chain. Furthermore, it is highly fragmented and relies heavily on interfaces where the industry and national governments come into direct contact—these interfaces are still often paper-based. Maersk, one of the largest shipping companies in the world, has been working to deploy blockchain and is already into its live trial process.

Telecom

The telecom industry sees enormous opportunity in blockchain. As one of the principal beneficiaries of the deployment of connected mobile devices to almost 4 billion people, telecommunication companies (telcos) are aware of just how enormous an opportunity may present itself if every device made by humans became connected—the internet of things and the sensor revolution. Without exception all major telcos are working on this topic. AT&T, British Telecom, Cisco, and Comcast have all been granted patents around this space.

Developing Markets

The examples just given are all drawn from developed economies and large corporations. However, there is at least as much innovation occurring in markets that are less well developed. Indeed, there is a fundamental reason why some countries are more inclined to become excited by, and become early adopters of, blockchain and cryptoassets. This is because some countries just don't have an existing trusted alternative.

Some places need to leapfrog the development process that the world's developed markets have passed through. As an example, if in Africa, there are no bank branches and ATMs, why wait for them to be installed before building out a modern payment system? Why not instead become a mobile-first-payments economy and directly move to a payment or banking system that does not rely upon traditional payment processes? This is what we see in countries like Kenya with BitPesa, and Ghana and Senegal with Atlas/ACX.

Mickey Costa, co-founder of Atlas/ACX, in his view as a blockchain entrepreneur explains, "It is best to always solve a real-world problem first and add blockchain after. Consumers need real solutions that give value, and blockchain can sometimes add to that but rarely provides that on its own. This is why Atlas took the approach of building an on-demand banking network first off-chain."

We fully expect that developing nations and those without secure and trustworthy monies will be the first to embrace and deploy cryptocurrencies and perhaps other blockchain-based solutions. Certainly we see a lot happening in these markets and derive a number of key insights and early best practices from observing what they are doing and experiencing.

From an investment perspective, Jalak Jobanputra of Future\ Perfect says, "I look for highly inefficient or unserved markets where blockchain technology can be implemented—I often think about the mobile money example in Kenya. The reason it took off before mobile banking came to the United States was that people there were unserved by banking institutions and willing to adopt a new behavior as it made their lives exponentially more productive."

Far from comprehensive, these are just examples of a global wave of work being conducted, with more coming as we begin to understand the impact that these innovations may have as we continue to evolve our digital economy.

This breadth and depth of large corporate engagement in a new area of technology has not been seen since the last transformative protocols were launched and the world got to grips with their implications during the rise of the internet—although the life sciences revolution and the consequences of the discovery of DNA, gene sequencing, and now gene editing are not far behind.

In the next chapter, we outline the other side of the coin—that adoption is not happening as fast as many had predicted and that there are very real barriers to be overcome.

Chapter 12
General Lack of Adoption

We tend to overestimate the effect of a technology in the short run and underestimate the effect in the long run.

—*Roy Amara*

Embedding an emerging technology into a competitive strategy does not come without its risks too. The world of startups is replete with examples where great teams with powerful future visions of how to compete were disappointed when the new technologies they were relying upon did not mature quickly enough to enable the startup to get their value propositions to market fast enough.

Early-stage investing is full of stories where investments failed because they ran out of capital before revenue could start to flow due to buggy software that just would not work the way it was promised. For established companies it is the very reason many avoid being at the "bleeding edge" of a new innovation. Often it is better to let others iron out the bugs and then sweep in once the adoption curve steepens even if valuations have begun to soar too. In this chapter, we explore some of the counter reasons why our readers should be careful before committing to a way to play that relies on a body of technology and innovation still in the steep early part of its development curve.

Hype vs. Adoption

All this activity does not quickly turn into massive adoption. Roy Amara wrote his "law" some years ago—"We tend to overestimate the effect of a technology in the short run and underestimate the effect in the long run." Some believe that in the case of blockchain we have done the reverse; however, first movers have found its adoption to be lagging.

Every day we read leading articles in major newspapers that declare the latest breakthrough in blockchain business without understanding that these examples have almost no usage. As examples:

- Lordless, a bounty hunter game based on the Ethereum protocol has a total of only 1,300 users at the time of writing and yet is the number-one decentralized application (DAPP) on Ethereum when measured by daily average users.

- Meanwhile, CryptoKitties declares itself the number-one blockchain "trading game" in the world and gets front-page coverage every day. However, only a handful of sales transactions occur per day.

- Lordless and CryptoKitties adoption levels are in marked contrast to the tens of millions of users and billions of dollars of revenue secured by leading conventional videogames like Epic Games' Fortnite, Riot Games' League of Legends, Mojang's Minecraft, and Supercell's Clash of Clans.

- Auger, the decentralized oracle and prediction market

protocol built on Ethereum, has been heralded as a breakthrough, but to date almost no activity has taken place on the platform.

More broadly it is fair to say that almost no projects have been moved out of development and into global production. Shifting from experiments into proven use cases that attract millions of paying users is still ahead of us.

Barriers to Adoption

There are a lot of barriers to adoption. Without going through them all a good starting list is that of global consultancy Deloitte:

- Time-consuming operations
- Lack of standardization
- High costs and complexity of blockchain applications
- Regulatory uncertainty
- Absence of collaboration between blockchain-related firms

For example, before blockchain-based solutions can cope with the demands of financial services transaction processing, the technology must greatly increase its speed, throughput, and peak capacity. Financial services networks operated by associations like Visa and Mastercard routinely handle transaction volumes several orders of magnitude larger than that currently afforded by the bitcoin protocol.

So too, interoperability is a major issue. Today we have thousands of unique blockchains that have been built to the specific and unique design of their founders. Making blockchains communicate with one another is a non-trivial task, and we are seeing the first steps to make this happen, both through the creation of standards and also through the building of interoperability layers like Interledger.

Regulatory uncertainty is a major issue, with different jurisdictions providing different guidance on what is and is not to take place. For startups the variability of regulations across jurisdictions is always a major source of friction to expansion. When the project begins with a global remit, the risk of breaking local rules rises to be a certainty. As a result, global harmonization of regulation will be a "to do" in coming years.

These are just examples, but they make the point that adoption is not only a matter of finding powerful use cases that end users embrace; it is also a matter of both the blockchain community and broader society getting up the curve and determining the consistent approaches and rules that can accelerate adoption.

To illustrate the divergent views on the likely course of blockchain adoption, two of the leading blockchain computer scientists—Joe Lubin of ConsenSys who was co-founder of Ethereum and Jimmy Song of Blockchain Capital—have entered into a bet around whether or not there will be any decentralized applications (DAPPs) over the next five years with significant usage. Joe Lubin offered to bet "any amount of bitcoin," but the details of the bet are still unresolved at the time of writing. It will be interesting to see who wins.

There are also structural issues that may slow adoption and these may actually be harder to resolve. We will briefly outline three of these: the flaw of exponential energy usage, the difficulty of managing protocols, and the rise of centralization. Each is now discussed in turn.

(Fatal?) Flaw of Exponential Energy Usage

The way the blockchains conduct their work is energy-intensive. At the extreme case of a truly open, distributed blockchain based upon a consensus proof-of-work algorithm, the energy usage can be intense. It is estimated by DigiEconomist that already just the bitcoin and bitcoin cash blockchains use more energy than Iraq and just a little less than Singapore, which makes them the 52nd largest energy user in the world were they a sovereign country—and they are still growing.

This is another non-trivial barrier that blockchain will need to overcome. Already the principal mining operations have relocated to low-energy-cost cold climates where their server farms can operate with lower costs—Northern China, Siberia, Iceland, and Norway. But that cannot be the ultimate answer. Today, we have not deployed any blockchain to even a fraction of the capacity required if the world truly embraced it for a digital money or a way to manage digital assets.

There are potential solutions being explored including truncation and archiving of blockchains so that each new block does not need to contain the full history of every block created to date, or private blockchains that don't required the massively copied blocks that an open, distributed network implies. So too researchers are looking at the proof-of-concept algorithm to see if other approaches can be created that still capture the benefits of the original bitcoin blockchain protocol while not giving up too many of the powerful advantages that Satoshi Nakamoto designed in.

We don't know where this will land. We hope necessity will prove to be the mother of invention and that blockchain will become less energy-intensive. Especially since the world's most challenging issue may actually be the environmental consequences of our hunger for power.

Difficulty of Managing Protocols—Herding Cats

Blockchains are built on the efforts of communities of people who to a large extent collaborate through incentives systems designed into the specific protocol around which they are working. One of the exceptionally brilliant aspects of the original bitcoin protocol was the way that it created collaboration between far-flung parties who had no knowledge of each other and no experience working together. It did this through the reward incentive baked into the consensus algorithm.

Unfortunately, getting people to collaborate together for long periods of time is never easy. We have seen minor points of difference and irritation over time turn into the rationale for going to war. The history of religion serves as a major headline in this regard.

Blockchain is already showing signs of stress as once like-minded individuals begin to prepare for war over their interpretations and beliefs about how blockchain should develop. This is of critical importance. Lou Kerner, co-founder and general partner at CryptoOracle, stated, "I think that the importance of community is still vastly under-appreciated by both most projects and investors."

The 2018 war between two forks (a fork is when the computer code of a blockchain is copied and split off to form a new branch from the original software. Forks allow for divergence over time of the two branches of the code) of bitcoin is a warning cry for what may yet be coming. Without rehashing the entire story, two factions of developers differed in their views on how bitcoin cash (BCH—itself a fork of bitcoin) should be evolved. One faction named Bitcoin Adjustable Blocksize Cap (BCH ABC) was spearheaded by proponents including Roger Ver and Jihan Wu, the co-founder of the blockchain unicorn Bitmain (a "unicorn" is the term for a private company with valuations exceeding US $1 billion), which is one of the largest blockchain mining companies in the world. This faction believed that BCH did not need any radical change. In the other side of the dispute was a group called Bitcoin Satoshi Vision (BCH SV) led by Craig Wright who claims that he is Satoshi Nakamoto.

In November 2018 the BCH blockchain was split, and each side began to try and demonstrate that their version was the better. Massive mining power was put to work, and a battle began. Of great concern were the threats that both sides began to make. Blockchain adoption requires that there be trust in the technology and in particular its immutability and integrity. Soon proponents of one of the forks began to threaten that they would damage the blocks of the other side by what is known as a 51% attack, which allows the attacker to essentially overwrite the historical blocks in the chain—changing history if you will.

The original concept of blockchain is that its distributed characteristic should make it impossible for any one party to gain

51% mining share. However, the rapid consolidation of the mining capacity into a few hands has made this now feasible. Indeed early in 2019 we saw a 51% attack successfully conducted against Ethereum Classic.

Who wins and who loses is not the concern here. The concern is that the very integrity is being undermined by the biggest proponents of the technology just as the world decides whether to deploy it to solve the internet's challenges.

In a very real sense, the blockchain community appears to be "cutting off its nose to spite its face."

Centralization Again—Pre-Mined, Pre-Owned

A logical and consequential concern of the prior section is the reappearance of centralization in power in what was originally intended to be a distributed innovation that grappled power away from narrowly defined and "self-serving" centralized authorities. Nakamoto mined one million bitcoins, and we do not know what happened to them. While giving away his innovation to the community and allowing anyone to share in the wealth, it is quite possible that Nakamoto is sitting somewhere in the world with billions of dollars made from what was heralded as a democratized digital money.

Blockchain protocols that have been developed since then have often been even more centralized. Much has been written regarding how some protocols issue a very large or even a majority of their tokens at launch to their own founders. EOS, Ripple, and Tron are mentioned in the press as examples. Post-launch the concentration of mining power also leads to continuing centralization of the benefits of blockchain protocols.

This is an issue worth following. Just how economic activity can be made beneficial to a large community when the core of the platform is owned by a few is a conundrum that we have seen before turn in favor of the few.

Good News—Continuous Innovation

A central theme of this book is that this is not the first time that we have seen a deployment of a new technology protocol that changed everything. Indeed the last 20 years of the internet's deployment hold many case studies, best practices, and analogies for the rollout of the blockchain protocol too.

Foremost among these is that the technology we begin with is not the technology we end up with. Few can forget the early days of online access. Arriving at Stanford Graduate School of Business (GSB) we were taught the essentials of going online. At the time, members of the Stanford Department of Computing and Information Management were beginning to provide online access to the students. These were the same people that would launch Cisco and deliver the servers and routers that would bring the internet to every business. However, back then the students used to log in from home to bid for courses at the beginning of each term and to check their class schedules.

The screens were monochrome (white and black, or green and black), the language was DOS, and it took forever to get the signal that would tell you that your computer was now on the network talking to the GSB mainframe. The pain associated with the slowness of the network, its limited use, and the frequent dropped connectivity can't be underestimated, especially if you really wanted to bid on Van Horne's seminar in corporate finance just as you lost the signal.

Later, ISPs like AOL and Prodigy made things better, but even then you waited forever to get text to download, and more often than not the connection could not cope with an image. Who can forget staring for minutes at the screen as a picture of the new baby in your family appeared on the screen, line by line, only to have it crash as the lines got down to the top of the eyes?

At the time, naysayers said that the internet would never work because of these issues of speed, throughput, and peak load capacity. Today we have real-time streaming video from anywhere in the world to almost anywhere else. Your child can be on a beach in Australia using FaceTime to chat to you when you are up a mountain in California. Who would have believed it?

Well, of course those are exactly the same technical challenges that blockchain has today. Without great advances in speed, throughput, and peak load capacity, among other things, we can't have effective, cost-efficient, and reliable native digital monies or assets.

Should we join the naysayers this time around and say that this will never work? We prefer to believe that continuous innovation is a hallmark of the way that the world works and that enough capital and talented people are now focusing on blockchain's shortcomings to be able to resolve these topics. And if not, the next Satoshi Nakamoto innovator will not be long in appearing.

Just as every big and important innovation discovers, when things become competitive within a space, those who have prepared to win are much more likely to. As a result, we focus for the rest of this book entirely on the issue of setting strategies for your way to play and using tactics to gain competitive advantage in a new and challenging world—whether you are an entrepreneur, investor, or established company.

Part III | Gaining Competitive Advantage

Chapter 13
Entrepreneur Advantage

Remembering that you are going to die is the best way I know to avoid the trap of thinking you have something to lose. You are already naked. There is no reason not to follow your heart.

—Steve Jobs

We will start our focus on the ways to gain competitive advantage by discussing it with reference to the entrepreneurs who are launching this blockchain revolution. They are the most important players in this story. They are few in number. The best are creative visionaries, capable leaders, driving managers, deeply knowledgeable in the technologies, focused and intense, unwilling to give up. Everything about innovation is built on their shoulders. They are born, not taught. They are hard to define. But once you meet one, you know you have met one.

If you are one of them, then this chapter is for you.

To think about competitive strategy as it applies to the entrepreneurs and the projects and companies they are leading, we begin with the realities they confront.

Most Blockchain Projects Will Fail

We are sorry to be the heralds of ill fortune. But in all areas of innovation, failure is the norm. The angel and venture-capital failure rates are between 55 and 65% even after these investors have done exhaustive due diligence and selected a few, out of hundreds, to back and then worked for years to help the teams they back make a go of it. The incubator/accelerator and crowdfunding failure rates are probably more than 90% though both are too new for the data to be robust.

How could we expect anything other than massive failure for the universe of blockchain projects? Even before we consider scams, plagiarized white papers, projects that, while worthy, never made any commercial sense, and so on.

By late 2018 the failure rate among the first wave of blockchain projects backed earlier in the years before had begun to spike. Deloitte believes that more than 50% of those early projects have already failed or been abandoned. In the next few years, most of the cryptoasset tokens will be abandoned or will crash in value. Even though there is an enormous need for these projects—the really good and deserving ones. Many of the failures will still create value. The teams and ideas will regroup and resurface in new and improved iterations. Such is the nature of innovation and evolution.

Bad News Comes First

Failure always comes first. In areas of new technology the initial barriers to entry are often low. Teams of entrepreneurs can say they plan to compete, and often investors, excited by the promise of a new technology, will seed them with the money they need to get started.

The complex realities of applying new technologies to make products and services that people really want only surface later.

And new markets only become competitive even later on. So the losers begin to drop out as they are confronted by these inevitable realities and as their money begins to run out. Those that are able to continue to play begin to show traction and in so doing are able to attract follow-on capital.

However, it takes a long time to move an established way of doing something to a fundamentally new technology or innovation. Let alone to do so while meeting a truly new or unmet need. Lots of trial and error. Each new wave building on the learnings of the last.

As we write this book, the shakeout has begun. In the next few years the bad news will be widespread, but that does not mean that the good news will begin to flow quickly. Expect that later. Investors understand how investment J curves work: the value of your investment capital actually drops in the first few years as you make investments, pay costs, and witness the first failures. Then the first exits begin to come in, and slowly the curve of your investment value begins to rise, crossing the break-even line and then moving into positive territory—most of the time. The good news begins once the surviving projects have created real businesses, and from there they either are able to reach the broader investment markets or are snapped up by established companies. And while the failures mean the investors are out of pocket, for the entrepreneurs there can be huge learning and growth even with failure. Many will go on to leverage what they have learned by regrouping in a new project or initiative. Fail fast, iterate, learn, get ever better and stronger.

Protocol Wars Are Beginning

Another reality facing entrepreneurs in the field is that we are about to see the first shots fired in what will become a global protocol war. What does this look like?

First, in software, it is a war for the best developers. There are only a finite number of blockchain developers, and the best can work anywhere they want. Protocols that make a compelling story to their developer community will pull ahead—attracting, and even raiding, the best developers, miners, and so on. Smarter protocols will make their story much more compelling than the others. We see this every day in software development where once strong players suddenly see an exodus as their key developers leave for greener pastures. For 20 years we have seen this in digital entertainment, where once blockbuster games suddenly are abandoned as the best game makers move to create new offerings (and by investing in videogames and virtual worlds we learned communities are fickle, and it's hard to make digital assets and virtual currencies cross the narrowly defined interests of specific publishers and game makers).

Second, expect feature expansion. Most protocols begin with a focus on something they want to do really well. Once they master that, they begin to add the features and foci of their principal competitors. If one protocol is good at smart contracts, then to compete a protocol that might be good at store of value may need to add smart contracts too. And vice versa.

Third, while sometimes this is organic feature expansion, often it happens by consolidation. The protocols that are beginning to pull ahead hoover up teams and even other projects to enhance their competitive position. The strong get stronger through canni-balization of the weak.

Fourth, if being a general-purpose protocol begins to look like a distant reality, then some protocols will instead focus on a niche strategy. They won't try and be good at everything. Instead they will drop back to trying to be the best at something narrower. Meeting the needs of a specific set of use cases, end users, developers, and so on, better than anyone else.

We don't know what the final shape of this will be. We suspect that there will only be a handful of general-purpose blockchain protocols in a few years' time supplemented by a few score niche protocols. But we are not sure. It could end up being only a handful of super capable general-purpose players (like in the areas of search or social), or it could go the other way completely with only those who master a specific area of application surviving. What we know for sure is that there won't be tens of thousands of valuable block-chain protocols in the end game—and we already have thousands.

Examining the top 20 blockchain protocols by market capital-ization, we already see some that have next to no developers work-ing on them. In the next few years expect more to be abandoned, and their values to collapse once the reality becomes obvious. Conversely, we are now seeing some very sophisticated leaders of protocol projects beginning to take actions to improve their com-petitive stance and prepare for this coming phase. We would call out Ripple and EOS as good examples of players who are working diligently to create ecosystems of partners and supporters to make sure that their protocols are actively supported and worked on. This work ranges from providing tools to developers, to making direct investments to support promising projects, to standing up dedicated venture firms to focus on supporting ecosystem projects and companies. Expect much more of this type of activity and also expect that the more passive protocols will also be those first abandoned by their communities.

Develop Your Strategy for Competitive Advantage

Given these realities of high failure rate, an early wave of failures, and a shift into a competitive phase, and without repeating the contents of the prior chapter, every blockchain entrepreneur and startup needs first to have a clear vision of the future and after that develop their own clear strategy within that context. As we outlined at the beginning of this book, developing competitive advantage in a fast-moving, disrupted industry requires different approaches than in established markets. It requires:

- A vision of the future and the big issues that need to be solved in that future
- A deep understanding of the enabling technologies you want to leverage
- A compelling way to play in the emerging ecosystem
- A clear understanding of the key success factors (KSFs)
- Plans for quickly securing a right to win

Without a sense of where they are heading and a compelling future view, projects will enter this competitive phase with a fuzzier starting point for developing a competitive advantage. Part I of this book describes a possible future view at the highest level and the challenges that need to be resolved to achieve it. This future view needs to be translated to be more relevant to your project or company and its focus. Part II describes the breakthrough blockchain and related technologies that can be leveraged to create that future. Most passionate blockchain entrepreneurs are quite familiar with the contents of these parts of this book. The work begins for them in developing a clear competitive strategy.

Establish Your Way to Play

It is important to articulate a compelling way to play—what it is the project or company is going to do and how it will deliver value—before cycling through the key success factors that need to be met and then developing a plan that secures a right to win. At the start-up or project level, the view of the future that you have needs to be translated into a clear way to play—specific to your project or company, its skills, interests, and what it is trying to achieve.

We described at the beginning of the book the shortcomings of traditional strategy development approaches in a world of new technologies and major disruption. Traditional approaches that start with analyzing existing markets, customer needs, and current competitor offerings simply don't work as well in phases of disruption. There are many approaches and tools for helping to develop your way to play, and in the introduction we describe a few of them—scenario planning, ecosystem mapping, disruptor analysis, and there are many others.

However, simple approaches can be just as effective. One such simple method is a brainstorming approach used with great success at eBay, Google, and PayPal as well as many smaller companies. We will call it "big ideas are born bad." It encourages a mindset and out-of-the-box thinking that is very valuable in creating competitive advantage in emerging, fast-moving, and uncertain opportunity areas and markets. The overall goal is to surface big ideas—many of which may be ugly or simply bad to start with—but may contain the seeds of something brilliant that no one has thought of yet.

First you need a group of people who won't go quickly to the negative; who are not trying to find weaknesses in an idea or reasons why it won't work; people who are not trying to score points for being able to find the faults in the ideas of others.

- You also need a diversity of people who see the world through different eyes and may be able to connect things in ways that others might not.
- Then you need a process that allows a lot of ideas to flourish and allows some people to build on the ideas of each other. Not in the sense of "let me build on what you said," but in a truly creative spirit where one person's spark is feely allowed to set light to another's. Ideally the process has plenty of time—sometimes over the course of several days or iterating over weeks.
- Next you need to let the ideas fly, and you record the really big ones—which will mostly be really big bad ideas.
- Once you have enough on the table, then you all work together to figure out how to make the big bad ideas into big good ones. Sometimes you split up the big bad ideas and actually task teams to come back with the best versions of each that they can imagine.

- Then the entire team must step back and create a set of criteria by which to rank and sort the remaining ideas. At this point you go from your open mindset to a more analytical approach.
- Finally, the top one to three big bold ideas for the company can be fleshed out and refined. The benefit of having spent time on more than one idea is that it explores corners and creates a broader view for possible pivots as the company moves forward and develops learnings.

In our experience it is easier to take a "big bad idea" and turn it into a "big good one" than to come up with a "big good idea" right from the start.

We have often worked with teams to facilitate these sessions, and it is incredible how the sense of clarity about what the company is going to focus on can improve. This sets an important stage for getting traction with investors, employees, and setting priorities with limited resources. As an example, at Google in the mid-2000s the big bad idea of "making the world's professional video content available to everyone" surfaced, and for awhile it became a way to play called Google Video. Eventually, the better big good idea of "making the world's video content available to everyone" without the restriction of only focusing on professional-grade video surfaced as the better idea. The Google team tried to build a right to win with this big good idea—only to find that by then it was better to buy YouTube than to try and compete with it. Similarly at eBay we facilitated offsites where the executive team of StubHub iterated their initial focus on a secondary market for just selling tickets, into a much bigger and broader proposition that allowed for a much more substantial relationship to ticket buyers.

Know the Key Success Factors

Assuming you have a compelling way to play, the challenge next is to be very clear on the key success factors (KSFs). A KSF is a critical element that is necessary for an organization or project to achieve its mission—those factors that will be most important to ensure that your chosen strategy or way to play can be translated into actions that quickly secure the right to win.

You would probably be surprised at how many teams we have seen that don't take the time to think through what they are or how many teams don't have a shared view of themselves. In the world of innovation where time, capital, and resources are scarce, not being crystal clear on your KSFs can be a fatal flaw for an early-stage business. It makes it hard to allocate scarce resources to the right things, to make the right tradeoffs, and to know when to pull the plug and pivot before it is too late.

Having spent time across a large number of blockchain projects and companies, we see a handful of common KSFs—although they may not all apply in your case and there may be others that are equally or more important. Common KSFs include the following:

- Focus on capability building (and the talent that matters).
- Grab best partners first.
- Play hard to stay ahead of competitors.
- Secure smart capital.
- Develop strong communities.

These are examples and some will likely be on the lists for most teams that go through this exercise. The KSFs for any company will depend on its chosen way to play and the dynamics of the field it is playing on. But let's go with these five KSFs and discuss how each of them can flow into actions required to quickly secure a right to win.

(Quickly) Secure a Right to Win

Importantly, as you flow from KSFs into the plan to turn your way to play into a right to win, what you are actually doing is creating tangible short-terms plans and tactics that establish your competitive advantage against each KSF. In a very practical sense, if you can do this and meet the KSFs faster and more completely than your competition, you almost always end up with a clear right to win. This is why clarity is so important. In our experience many strategy efforts can get very bogged down in the weeds of minutiae and complex analysis that only end up being confusing or slowing down decisions. Know your KSFs for your chosen way to play and start to execute on a plan that delivers them with speed and agility. The next few pages illustrate this with the common KSFs we described earlier.

Focus on Capability Building

For those companies and projects that make it into the competitive phase, the emphasis will shift from technology to building out the important broader capabilities required to compete. The reality has already set in. The early euphoria of a white paper and fundraising campaign is now being replaced by the hard reality of building the products and services that were promised to the community that backed the project. It is easy to say that a new technology will change the world. It is easy to find a big current challenge or unmet need that really should be solved. It is also easy to combine the two and say that you will solve a world problem with a new (blockchain) technology.

However, actually bringing products to the point that they are ready for real-world use, convincing users to try your offering, making sure the customer experience is a positive one, aligning existing players—channels, outlets, service partners, etc.—to support the new offering, all requires a huge amount of work. Many teams give up when they realize that concept and reality are not the same thing—for many the work needed to make something real will prove to be beyond their capabilities—or just not that attractive to commit themselves to.

Every blockchain project backed prior to 2018 began with the proposition that new technology would be able to meaningfully make the world a better place. In almost every case, the people who made those claims and wrote those white papers were technologists.

Building a global technology business is about more than technology. Supporting a global community is about more than open-source technology development and a motivated community. Every use case, every potential product and service, will require a host of other capabilities.

Which ones should you focus on? The answer flows directly from the vision and strategy process we outlined. The KSFs that you identified also define the capabilities that you must focus on securing. If you were, for example, building a global blockchain-enabled investor platform built upon security tokens, then the KSFs are going to be: one, capturing a critical mass of accredited investors on your platform; two, ensuring that you have access to high-quality, attractive investments; and three, making sure that your platform is comprehensive, integrated, and easy to use.

The capabilities you need to focus on flow from this. You have to move quickly to be good at signing up the investors and sourcing the deal flow. Additionally, you have to build that seamless platform quickly. Across all three, the questions of make versus buy/partner become important to resolve quickly. Because if you decide to buy/partner, you may well find that the best third parties are few in number, and once your competitors also see that, there will likely be a scramble to secure access—a scramble that will leave a few with what they were looking for and a much larger number left without seats at the table.

To use an example to illustrate this in practice, take a look at the actions Coinbase is taking to move itself ahead of competing wallet and exchange players. While operating in an entirely regulatory compliant fashion has in some ways slowed Coinbase down, they have proven adept at knitting together a powerful strategy for competing. In the Coinbase case they are based in the US where the rules regarding investment are well established, compliance is monitored, and actors are penalized when found not to be following the rules. This has meant that Coinbase simply can't move as fast or take all the risks that an offshore player like Binance is able to take. However, Coinbase has been sophisticated in establishing a network of relationships with others. For example, the Coinbase venture-capital arm has been very active in supporting tokenization players with the understanding that future business will be directed towards their wallets where appropriate. The recent announcement that Coinbase invested in the Securitize fundraising round is an illustration of an action taken to establish a potential on-ramp partnership.

There are likely other areas of capability included in KSFs and that need to be built to differentiate your company and ensure traction. Recent problems at companies like Tesla, Theranos, Uber, and Zenefits illustrate what can go wrong when a fast-growth disruptive technology company does not build critical capabilities in areas such as these:

- Sales
- User experience
- Marketing
- Account management
- Customer service
- Operations and logistics
- Community engagement
- Regulatory and government affairs
- Finance
- Talent management
- And so on

These functions and capabilities are the focus of the majority of the workforce at technology leaders like Amazon, Apple, Google, and others. So too, we expect in the future ecosystems that will surround communities like bitcoin, EOS, and Ethereum, and in the emerging companies like Abra, Coinbase, Ripple, and Securitize. The balance of work will begin to shift from technology, to building global communities and businesses that can excel in go-to-market and driving adoption and usage.

Being good at much more than technology will be essential to compete successfully.

Grab Best Partners First

In chapter 10, we talked about the lessons learned from observing how the best corporations navigated the arrival of the internet. One of the best practices we described was moving quickly to lock in the best disruptive companies as soon as they became apparent. In the next chapter on investor advantage, we will show how smart venture investors also work hard to connect their portfolio companies together to create competitive advantage.

There is a parallel strategy for entrepreneurs and the projects and companies they lead. Once you are clear on the KSFs and once you know what you will make and what you need to buy/ partner for, it is important to move quickly to lock up the best large companies before your competitors can do so.

So if you determine, for example, that your specific project needs go-to-market partners (and most do), then it typically is the case that only a few great partners exist who have the access and capabilities that may be critical. The projects that partner with those players early often are able to hold off incursions from late arrivals. We are seeing this type of strategy already in blockchain. For example, Abra and Bitwise partnered so that the former has a great family of investment products for their investors and the latter has additional distribution—both companies being backed by the same venture-capital firms.

This flurry of early partnerships takes place in a setting that will eventually become a zero-sum game in most cases. If large corporations have chosen disruptive technology partners, committed resources to work with them, and made the internal decisions to work together to take new products and services to existing customers, those decisions will not usually be reversed quickly. The same is even more true with emerging unicorns who have even less capacity to support lots of time-consuming partnerships. This means that for at least one or two rounds of the game, those players will not be available to other disruptive companies.

A very good example of this is the action taken by Ripple to ensure that an enormous network of large banks were partnered early in exploring and prototyping applications of the Ripple protocol and initial use cases. Those banks, which did not sign non-competes or exclusivity clauses, nonetheless have become much more reticent to sign similar partnership agreements with other protocol players. The refrain—"We already have a similar partnership with Ripple and don't need another"—is likely to be heard in every first meeting between the Ripple partner banks and competing protocol teams.

Being a first mover in capturing your go-to-market partners is one example of how to gain competitive advantage in most industries that blockchain will be applied to.

Play Hard to Stay Ahead of Competitors

If the suggestion mentioned above of cannibalizing the developer communities of your competitor protocols does not already sound like hard ball, consider some of the following other competitor strategies that are widely used in traditional industries and traditional competitive software markets:

- Aggressively pursuing your competitors most important clients and users
- Poaching the best talent; offering a better talent value proposition for critical hires
- Undermining competitors' pricing strategies
- Attacking competitors' economic profit pools
- Launching copyright and IP protection campaigns
- Filing legal, competitive, or regulatory cases against competitors where merited

The list is long. We are not suggesting for a moment anyone should do anything illegal, unethical, or against their principles. Nor are we suggesting that you should engineer a 51% attack against your competitor protocol to get it dropped by exchanges and put out of business. But we do suggest you have your eyes open to what intense competition will make some competitors do.

When survival is the objective, people begin to compete much less graciously. The "we are all in this revolution together" mindset gets replaced by a "my team and community has got to survive" mindset. As such, the feasible set of competitive tactics and strategies changes as that mindset shift takes place.

Expect to see the leading projects and protocols act more competitively and less collaboratively as we move into this new competitive phase.

Secure Smart Capital

By the end of 2018 it became apparent that raising capital, which seemed so easy in 2017 and the first half of 2018, was no longer sufficient to help a project win.

In traditional technology investing we know that capital is only enough to get started and to fund the engine you build. "Smart capital" brings resources, skills, connections, and advice to help the investee companies set strategy, build capabilities, and drive market momentum. The best technology venture-capital firms, like Andreessen, Greylock, Draper, RRE, and Sequoia, are successful only partially because they have capital. As Sequoia puts it, "We are good at building public companies."

In blockchain, the hundreds of crypto hedge funds that were stood up over the last two years will begin to shake out as the collapse in cryptoasset valuations shows up in their performance—most of the traditional hedge funds that moved into crypto are not value-added investors (they are traders), and most of them have funds that allow redemption. We will see a flight of capital from most of them with a handful of better funds surviving.

More importantly, the value of the long-term investors in blockchain will become apparent. The best blockchain venture investors, like 1confirmation, Blockchain Capital, Castle Island, CryptoOracle, Future\Perfect, IDEO CoLab Ventures, and Pantera, to name just seven in the US, and 1kx and Fabric in Europe, will become apparent because of the added value they provide to the companies they back (Sidebar 9). Meanwhile, the funds that just bring capital will be, and should be, avoided by the best teams and the best projects. As observed by Dan Elitzer of IDEO CoLab

Ventures, "In this [blockchain] industry, while capital is rarely a constraint, everyone is eager to find values-aligned partners who can help bootstrap networks and work with teams to achieve product-market fit."

Sidebar 9: Advantages of Blockchain Pure-Play Funds

As discussed in the analysis of learnings from the internet dot-com boom and bust, one of most important trends was the formation of new venture firms focused on investing in and supporting the growth of new disruptive internet businesses. These firms became the winning investors of the period, and many of them are today among the largest venture investors in the world.

The blockchain phase of internet evolution is seeing the formation of a similar new family of venture firms but this time ones that chose to be "pure-play" blockchain investors.

1. **What It Is**—pure-play investors focus entirely on a subset of all areas of emerging technology and innovation. Typically they do so by focusing either on an industry vertical (e.g., Lifesciences) or a technology (e.g., CRISPR). In this case, the focus is on blockchain and/or cryptoassets.

2. **Benefits of Pure Play**—the principal benefits of being a pure-play investor are the following:

a. By focusing on a relatively narrow space it is easier to accumulate deep expertise and the key competencies required to make sound investment decisions.

b. Such a focus also provides the development of deeper relationships with entrepreneurs, investors, companies, regulators, etc., in the given space—relationships which can be leveraged to the benefit of portfolio companies.

c. Pure-play venture firms may also develop relationships between one another to create an "inside circle" of investors who are similarly focused and who may syndicate their best deals to make sure there is sufficient capital and support within the community within which they operate.

d. The position of visible leadership that is then created within the space feeds on itself as the best entrepreneurs and investment opportunities will naturally go first to the focused venture firms in the space.

3. **Disadvantages**—the principal disadvantages of pure-play venture firms are that they are more exposed to the potential downs in their narrowly defined investment focus (they don't have the

cross-space diversification of broader general-purpose firms). They may have less ability to mobilize players in other industries who may be needed to deploy portfolio company offerings into other adjacent industries and technologies.

4. **Leaders**—within blockchain there are a handful of leading pure-play investors surfacing. First among these in the US are Blockchain Capital and Pantera Capital, both of which became active in the 2013 and 2014 timeframe and both have now been joined by other firms, including 1confirmation, Castle Island, CryptoOracle, Future\Perfect, and IDEO. In Europe we see the establishment of focused blockchain venture firms such as 1kx and Fabric now taking place.

In order to secure access to these and other leading blockchain long-term investment funds, we—Alison and Matthew—have created a blockchain fund of funds. For full disclosure our investment strategy includes investing in all of the firms mentioned above.

If you are a blockchain entrepreneur, convince the best investors to back you. This could be the single move that most greatly raises the probability of your success.

Develop Strong Communities

There is one way in which blockchain is quite different from many areas of technology innovation: its reliance upon broad communities of common purpose, especially when the blockchains are open rather than private.

Starting with the open-source software development communities of the 1990s, a lot of software has been written by people who don't formally work together in the same company but who chose to work together in the same project. They often are held together by common interests, common values, or incentive systems that bring them together. Hunter Horsley, CEO of Bitwise and a former Facebook executive, describes the phenomenon in this way, "Public blockchains are more like Facebook than Intel. They derive advantage and defensibility from network effects rather than proprietary IP. Thus, go-to-market is the essential task development teams should focus around."

First standing up and then keeping aligned and motivating a large community of individual actors is very hard to do. As time goes by, we have frequently seen communities that once seemed strongly aligned begin to fragment and dissolve. As just one example in gaming, large global communities of users and co-creators—often in the hundreds of thousands or even millions—working together in virtual worlds, like Runescape, Habbo Hotel, Guild Wars—have been seen to suddenly vaporize as a more attractive environment appears. Leaving behind only hard-core loyalists, plus those with so much vested interest that they are reticent to depart.

For blockchain protocols that rely upon long-term maintenance of large and motivated communities, a new capability will become paramount: community preservation. Dan Elitzer of IDEO CoLab Ventures noted, "In an industry where it is often a functional requirement that code be open-source, it is even more important to build a strong brand and passionate community around your project. It is easy to fork code; it is hard to replicate community."

Pivoting If You Can't Secure a Right to Win

Can we guarantee that you will have secured a right to win if you do have a clear plan for addressing the top five (or three or 10) KSFs that you surface as critical in the context of your chosen way to play?

No we can't. But we do know you will have a better strategic plan than 95% of the other blockchain projects and companies that we have interacted with. After that, you have to be pragmatic.

If you still can't see yourself being able to beat one or maybe a handful of other competitors who have also chosen your way to play and who have also met the requirements of the KSFs, then probably it is time to pivot. This means going back to the beginning of this chapter and picking your second best way to play and going through all the steps one more time. Except by now, not only may you have learned enough to be able to define additional and perhaps better ways to play, you should also have built some tangible advantages that will help accomplish a different right to win—although stranded elements of old strategies inevitably surface when companies pivot and it is a real discipline to abandon (or sell or give away) things that once seemed so important but now are entirely irrelevant to a new competitive strategy.

In summary, for a blockchain entrepreneurial team it makes sense to get ahead of the competitive battle by thinking it through early. Within a broad future vision enabled by emerging block-chain technologies, create a big bold way to play for your company. Know how you will leverage innovation and new technologies to make it a reality, but even more importantly understand the other KSFs that your chosen way to play will rely upon and the approach you will take to establish them. Then move quickly to put as much space as possible in place between your own project and those that will become your competitors' and secure your right to win.

Competitive advantage is not easily won. However, we are beginning to see the drivers of gaining that advantage. Paul Vera-dittakit, general partner at Pantera, emphasizes, "Projects can get an advantage through building regulatory moats, building a strong community, and enabling a new use case that couldn't have been done before using the blockchain."

In the next chapter, we view the same challenge from the in-vestor perspective. We recommend that entrepreneurs keep read-ing. Knowing what your investors want is one way of improving your chances of getting funding from them. After that we will turn to look at competitive advantage for established companies—and the same will be the case. If you seek to get a larger company to throw its weight behind your project and company as a partner or customer (rather than behind your competitors), it is important to understand what they care about. We often see technology entre-preneurs so passionate about their work that they have completely forgotten that in relationships you have to begin by worrying first about what the other partner needs and values.

Chapter 14
Investor Advantage

There's nothing more invigorating than being deeply involved with a small company and a young team of founders out to do something incredibly special.

—Michael Moritz

If entrepreneurs are in the driving seat of blockchain technology innovation, they all have some investors in the backseat who have rented the car and paid for the gas. The very best ones have an investor alongside them ready to give input on navigation if asked to do so and help push the car over a steep hill if needed. Fortunately the investors often do very well by being on the journey.

In this chapter, we will focus on the best practices for being an investor in early-stage technology companies and how to apply these best practices to make it much more likely you will capture competitive advantage when investing in blockchain projects and companies.

Returns Exceptionally High

Despite (or perhaps because of) the inefficiency in private equity investing discussed earlier in the book, the returns to investors are exceptionally high for those who know how to play. Matthew's former partner at Monitor Group, Tom Copeland, was a leader in academic research on valuation and efficient market theory, and we remember well his lessons. What particularly comes to mind in the writing of this book is his observation that while markets that have access to an abundance of transparent information and many players, tend towards market efficiency, markets in which there is no access to public information and where only a few sellers and buyers interact are likely to show inefficiency with the possibility of superior returns.

Early-stage private equity investing is at the extreme of being characterized by opaqueness, lack of information, and small numbers of buyers and sellers. We have written elsewhere on this topic in our book *Build your fortune in the fifth era.* Sidebar 10 summarizes some of the academic findings on the expected returns of investing in private equities of early-stage technology companies.

Sidebar 10: Expected Return of Angel Investors in Groups

Angel investors back more than 71 thousand businesses each year in the US and many hundreds of thousands more around the world. These are most frequently technology-enabled businesses and are seen to be important drivers of innovation, GDP, and job growth by most countries worldwide. And while there is little academic research into angel investors, those researchers in this space have found:

- The return to angels investing in groups is viewed as attractive and perhaps as high as net annual internal rate of returns (IRRs) in the mid-twenty percents.
- In their groundbreaking 2002 research, Mason and

Harrison in the UK showed that angels have a signifi-
cantly lower number of exits (a positive exit being a
sale or public offering of a company in most cases)
that return no capital (39.8% as compared to 64.2%
for VCs), have a larger number that return modest
IRRs, and have roughly comparable proportions of
exits showing IRRs exceeding 50% (angels 23.5% of
deals; VCs 21.5% of deals).

Angels achieve their returns with relatively low failure rates
and lots of modest returns, adding to the return of the
relatively infrequent large exits. Mason and Harrison also
showed that technology deals outperform non-technology
deals in their period of assessment.

- Professor Robert Wiltbank, working with the sup-
  port of the Kauffman and Angel Capital Education
  Foundations in the US in 2007 and the British
  Business Angels Association in the UK in 2009,
  showed that:
  - Angels can expect an average return of 2.6 times
    their investment in 3.5 years for a 27% IRR in
    the US.
  - Angels can expect an average return of 2.2 times
    their investment in just under four years for a
    22% IRR in the UK.
- George Roach (2008) conducted focused research
  on the world's largest angel group, Keiretsu Forum.
  His assessment of annual angel investor returns

provides very similar findings. By 2008, the annualized returns for the cohorts in the Keiretsu Forum portfolio were 2000—20.38%, 2001—21.32%, 2002—28.24%, 2003—26.20%, 2004—32.46%, 2005—14.55%, and 2006—20.13%.

The returns given in the previous bullet point arrive over a three- to five-year timeframe with a tail of investments that may take longer to realize. The successful exits tend to be less skewed than the venture-capital experience, but nonetheless a majority of the total return is still returned by a small number of highly successful outcomes. While this makes the average angel return attractive, it also implies that a significant number of angel investors may still have portfolios that do not perform, and, in fact, many angels do not see a return of capital. The most practical way for an angel to raise the likelihood of capturing the angel return is to ensure they are highly diversified in terms of the number of companies they hold in their portfolio. If they have a specific industry or sector focus, then the same applies at that specific level too.

Angels understand both the attractive returns possible and the need for diversification. However, angels are limited in their ability to achieve diversification. In practice, most invest in far fewer early-stage technology companies than preferable.

Source: Le Merle, M., & Davis, A. (2017). *Build your fortune in the fifth era*. Cartwright Publishing.

Lessons from the Dot-Com Boom and Bust

The first phase of the enablement of our digitally connected world was perhaps the greatest wealth accumulation event that the world has ever seen. In our other books we have detailed both the scale and extent of this value creation as well as the reality that most investors missed out. Ironically, the latter continues to be true since more than 97% of US accredited households do not invest in early-stage technology companies as either angels or venture capitalists. The same can be said of established companies where even 20 years on, most established companies are still not at the forefront of the technologies that are transforming their industries and businesses, and often the best digital world innovators continue to be disruptive players.

There are several indicators of this wealth creation. For example, the uppermost ranks of the most valuable companies are now filled with technology companies like Alibaba, Alphabet, Amazon, Apple, Facebook, Microsoft, and Tencent. The "wealthiest people" lists are now dominated by first-generation technology entrepreneurs. Also, the asset class returns are highest in early-stage technology where—after costs—venture capitalists average 32% IRRs, thus far outpacing the low single-digit long-term returns of fixed income and the high single-digit returns of the public equity markets.

What did investors learn from investing in the dot-com boom? There are some key lessons that any blockchain investor would do well to heed. Here are seven of those lessons.

One—Value Was Captured Early

Unlike in prior periods where late-stage investors could still hope to gain the benefits of expanding technologies around the world once they had been proven in one region, the wealth creation of internet technologies was, and continues to be, captured early by the entrepreneurs themselves and by the investors who back them. Indeed, in the last few years this phenomenon has been accentuated as technology companies have postponed entering the public markets and ever-larger rounds have been raised from private sources.

To show how important this phenomenon is, consider the returns of the venture-capital investors. Here, while the 25-year return is an IRR of 24% according to Cambridge Associates, the VCs earned only 12% IRR from their late-stage investment rounds but an incredible 32% IRR from their early-stage rounds.

The take-away: it is critically important to invest early to capture the highest returns from disruptive innovations.

Two—Follow On Investing Reduced Returns

The corollary of this finding is that it can reduce your returns to follow on invest in later rounds if you are already an investor in a fast-growth company. Of course the rounds are getting larger, so an investor can get more money to work, but as the VC returns above show, it makes more sense to invest early and not follow on than invest in every round, if the goal is the highest return rather than the largest absolute gain or the highest fees on money invested.

Three—Inside Deals and Circles Won Big

This is a key observation that we will return to throughout this chapter.

In the dot-com phase a few very active and connected VCs dominated the investing in what would become the internet unicorns and eventually the public companies that sit at the top of the rankings of market capitalization today. Those investors tended to work together and a virtual "inside circle" formed. We see this today in the unicorn lists where a small number of VCs, including Andreessen Horowitz, Draper, Kleiner Perkins Caufield & Byers (KPCB), New Enterprise Associates (NEA), and Sequoia, each have 20 and more unicorns while of the US's over 1,000 venture funds, 95% of them do not even have one.

This dominance of the best opportunities was not only a matter of being in the right place at the right time. Rather, as noted in the prior chapter, this inside circle of investors was also very capable at assisting their companies become leaders in their chosen fields by bringing knowledge, relationships, and capabilities to bear. In addition, and more subtly, the inside circle of investors connected their portfolio companies together to help them pull ahead. So, as an example, Excite (funded by IDG, IVP, and KPCB) was merged with @Home (funded by KPCB), which was then sold to Yahoo! (funded by Andreesen and Sequoia).

It is common sense in a way that the leaders would act like this. Their opportunity is not so much won at the cost of one another; it is won by a share shift against the entire established world of companies and industries, so collaboration between the inside circle of investors is a smart strategy if their fragile disruptive portfolio companies are to get over the finish line.

Four—New Blue Chip Investors Surfaced

At the outset of the internet revolution there was no shortage of large private equity investors in financial centers like New York's Wall Street or England's City of London. However, it clearly became apparent that these investors, more focused on Industrial Era companies and lacking in the skills to identify and assist new innovative teams, were not fit for the task of investing in pre-revenue, loss-making internet protocol companies.

Instead we saw the rapid emergence of a new breed of venture-capital firms that have gone on to raise ever-larger funds until they have the capital to invest from the early stage all the way to the IPO should they chose to do so. We have mentioned some of their names in the prior section. Suffice to say that these blue chip investors rode the wave of the internet to become among the largest and highest-performing investors in the world.

Five—Flight to Quality after Crash

After the dot-com crash, a large percentage of venture-capital funds were no longer able to raise capital and in practice became "walking dead." That is to say, because of their 10-year lifecycles, their existing funds continued in existence, but without new money the venture capitalists often could not make additional investments. They sat on the management fee, oversaw their existing portfolio, and hoped that a few good exits might get them to an acceptable return whereby they might be considered investable once again.

The other side of that same coin was that new capital quickly focused on gaining access to the inside circle of high-performing venture firms. This flight of capital to the blue chip firms made them ever-larger but also more exclusive.

Six—Access Diminished Over Time

When a firm like Andreessen Horowitz was first launched, it was possible to be an individual investor in it. Firms needed capital, and even small investors might have an opportunity to be limited partners, especially if they had a relationship with the general partners. Over time as these firms raised larger and larger funds, so their minimum investment also rose until most of them only accepted institutional investors who could put a minimum investment of millions of dollars to work.

However, while the funds closed their doors to individuals and family offices, in many cases honor was paid to the investors who had supported the firm at inception. Today most of the leading venture-capital firms will have parallel vehicles for their friends and loyal investors while their new funds are otherwise closed to smaller investors.

Seven—Funds of Funds Provided Access

Given these dynamics, the end of the dot-com phase also saw the rise of a new breed of fund of funds focused on providing access to the inner circle of venture-capital funds. Names like Greenspring, Horsley Bridge, and Top Tier Capital surfaced providing access through 1% and 10% fund-of-funds models (1% annual management fee and 10% carried interest).

For most investors, including overseas and family office investors, these funds of funds were often the only way to access the top-tier venture-capital firms. Unfortunately, funds of funds also wanted to get larger by raising more and more capital, so many chose to "dilute" their portfolios with firms whose performance was not likely to be top quartile. Investors in funds of funds often find that when they look closely, the top-tier funds that provide the sizzle in the prospectus only represent a small percentage of the total capital allocated whereas lesser-known firms may often represent the vast majority of the assets.

Implications for Blockchain Investing

These learnings from the dot-com era provide important KSFs for investing into the blockchain protocol (and indeed for early-stage technology investing in general). They imply:

- Avoid the herd
- Avoid high valuations
- Avoid publicly shopped deals
- Avoid unknown players
- Avoid market-timing strategies

Instead:

- Invest in early-stages (equity and/or tokens)
- Access "insider" investors/funds
- Get in early to emerging venture-capital stars
- Diversify given risk profile
- Consider quality fund of funds

Let's now take a closer look at what is happening within the block-chain space.

What Investment Advisors Are Advocating

The first place to look to see how the investment community is reacting to the emergence of a new asset class is always to read the work of the most influential institutional investors and investment advisors. These are the firms that influence the allocation of billions and in some cases trillions of dollars of assets. Firms like Blackrock, Fidelity, and Goldman Sachs all have very different businesses, but each has trillions of dollars in assets under management. Meanwhile, advisory firms like Cambridge Associates have a very important voice across the investment landscape especially in the US. Beyond these influencers we also see some institutions that are viewed by others as being particularly astute at spotting new investment opportunities. Among educational endowments in the US, Yale has long held this position especially with regard to emerging and private asset categories.

What are these players recommending to their investors and clients? Here are their respective views at the time of writing this book although it must be said that sentiment appears to be shifting quickly as more and more large financial institutions follow the 180-degree reversal of JPMorgan where the CEO Jamie Dimon spent most of 2018 saying bitcoin was a fraud before announcing in early 2019 that he was proud to be launching his own version of bitcoin—JPM Coin.

- Blackrock is the largest asset management company in the world with over US $6 trillion under management. In the summer of 2018 its CEO Larry Fink was quoted as saying, "I don't believe any client has sought out crypto exposure" and "I've not heard from one client who says, 'I need to be in this.'" Despite establishing a working team to monitor the space, Blackrock has not to date done anything significant in the space.

- Cambridge Associates is the Boston-based investment advisory consulting firm to the pension and endowment industry of the US. As a result, when they take a point of view, it can be very influential. Estimates are that Cambridge has more than US $380 billion under advisement and US $30 billion in assets under management. In early 2019 Cambridge Associates published a report called "Cryptoassets," which concluded, "It is worthwhile for clients to begin exploring the cryptoasset area today, with an eye toward the future." More specifically, the report profiles three investment strategies and appeared to be most favorably inclined towards the third:

  1. The public index approach uses indexes to gain exposure to mainstream cryptoassets, offering the most liquid and "hands-off" approach to crypto investing.

2. The public active approach targets market inefficiencies in hopes of outperforming public index
   approaches involving both fundamental and technical long/short strategies.

3. The private equity approach matches typical ven-
   ture-capital-style strategies that aim to align LP
   and GP incentives with fund structures that limit
   the taking of business risk in order to promote a
   longer-term investment focus.

- Fidelity, also based in Boston, manages more than US
  $2.5 trillion for its clients. Chairman and CEO Abigail
  Johnson has been a vocal proponent of blockchain and
  has created a strategy for Fidelity to be a leader in cryptoasset custody on behalf of its worldwide clients. Fidelity has also been an active equity investor in blockchain
  startups. Johnson underlines, "We are not in a hurry, and
  we want to do this right."
- Goldman Sachs, one of the largest investment banking
  firms in the world, includes primary dealing, market
  making, prime brokerage, and securities underwriting
  businesses, all of which are beginning to be impacted
  by blockchain initiatives. Goldman has been cautiously
  positive on blockchain and has been assisting its clients
  invest and trade in cryptoassets and derivatives, and,
  like Fidelity, has been making equity investments into
  the space.

- The Yale endowment, with almost US $30 billion under management, has been a leader in finding high-returning private investment strategies over the last few decades. CEO David Swenson has recently committed the endowment to cryptoasset investing including two significant limited partner positions in Andreessen Horowitz's new US $300 million crypto fund and Paradigm's new blockchain and crypto fund. Paradigm's founders are Coinbase co-founder Fred Ehrsam and former Sequoia partner Matt Huang.

These are examples of course. However, these voices are very powerful ones, and there appears to be growing sentiment that cryptoassets are ready for cautious investment. Fidelity recently completed its own report looking at how US and international institutional investors view artificial intelligence and blockchain. The findings were that 73% of the investors surveyed believe that these technologies will have a big role in the investment industry allocation decisions over the next seven years.

First Wave of Blockchain Unicorns

From a private equity investor's perspective (Cambridge's third investment approach), we are seeing exciting momentum build in the blockchain equity investment arena. While the ICO wave peaked and crashed in 2018, the capital flowing into the sector greatly increased through traditional venture and private equity investing.

Partially this reflects an expansion of players active in the space. The pioneering pure-play venture-capital firms that we have already profiled have been joined by some of the best general-purpose firms that have made substantial allocations to the space.

In addition, we have seen a handful of firms "eat their own dog food" in the sense that they have created tokenized investment funds. The first in the world was Blockchain Capital's BCAP (Sidebar 11), joined shortly after by Spice Ventures' tokenized fund—both on the Securitize platform. Others have begun to line up to create similar products.

Sidebar 11: Blockchain Capital's BCAP

Blockchain Capital was the first blockchain pure-play venture-capital firm, founded in San Francisco by Bart and Brad Stephens and Brock Pierce in 2013. Brock has now moved on to other areas of focus including EOS, so the firm's third general partner is now Spencer Bogart. The firm has raised three traditional venture funds, which have invested in more than 75 blockchain companies and projects, including notable names such as Abra, BitPesa, Bitwise, Coinbase, Filecoin, Kraken, Ripple, and Securitize, to name just a handful. For full disclosure, Alison is chairman of the advisory board at Blockchain Capital.

As a leader in blockchain investing, the team at Blockchain Capital decided in 2017 to also create a fund that fully leveraged the possibilities of blockchain and tokenization. This new approach to raising capital consisted of a fungible cryptoasset called BCAP that is operated on the Securitize compliance platform leveraging the Ethereum blockchain. The capital raised through the sale of the token is invested by

Blockchain Capital into blockchain projects and companies.

BCAP is in essence the first ever tokenized venture-capital fund. Today other venture-capital firms have issued tokenized funds including City Block and Spice VC, and many more are watching the space.

At the time of launch, Brad Stephens explained the importance of BCAP as the first venture-capital fund that could also offer liquidity. He said, "My phone is blowing up with other VCs saying, 'I want to do this,' because the biggest problem with venture, the thing everyone hates about venture capital, is that it's delivered fantastic returns, but no one wants to invest in an asset that's locked up for 10 years or more. The idea you can invest in a venture fund and have liquidity is probably the most innovative thing that has ever happened in the history of the venture-capital industry."

These early pure-play blockchain venture funds have been investing in early blockchain projects for a few years now, and we have begun to see the emergence of the first large rounds pushing the valuations of some of the portfolio companies into the territory of unicorns—private companies with valuations exceeding US $1 billion. Examples of this phenomenon of rounds in the hundreds of millions of dollars include Andela, Bitmain, and Coinbase. In addition, we have the blockchain projects that raised vast amounts of capital through their ICO offerings in these ranks—including EOS, Ethereum, Ripple, and Telegram. Many other unicorns that were not born as blockchain companies are now deploying the technology into their businesses. Some are entirely pivoting to focus on the area—Overstock being a good example of this, with its creation of a comprehensive blockchain-enabled strategy including the creation of tZero, its online exchange for cryptoassets.

Should the reader wish to participate as a blockchain investor, what are their options? What are the possible ways to play?

Pick an Investment Way to Play

In our earlier book, *Build Your Fortune in the Fifth Era*, we outlined in full the ways to play for early-stage investors and provided a structured thought process for deciding which option is your best fit given your particular objectives, goals, capabilities, and assets. In that book the nine options presented are the following, of which options three to seven are the investor options:

- Option 1. Technology Entrepreneur
- Option 2. Employee of a Fifth Era Company
- Option 3. Active Investor: Venture-Capital Fund
- Option 4. Passive Investor: Venture-Capital Funds
- Option 5. Active Investor: Angel Investor
- Option 6. Passive Investor: Angel Co-Investment Funds
- Option 7. Crowdfunding Investor
- Option 8. Provider of an Incubator and/or Accelerator
- Option 9. Provider of Professional Services to Fifth Era Companies

These options apply just as much to blockchain investing as they do to other early-stage technology investing. We would highlight that it simply becomes a little more difficult because some of the options are less well populated than will be the case in a few years time. So in Options 3 and 4 there are simply a lot fewer teams capable of leading a blockchain venture firm (Option 3), and so there are also less "inside circle" pure-play blockchain venture-capital funds for limited partners to invest in (Option 4). Meanwhile, in a new and emerging space, Options 5, 6, and 7 all raise the prospect that you may have to build expertise and access to those pioneers who understand how to use a technology even though few do. You may also find yourself investing with and into bad deals brought by bad actors who have not yet been flushed out by investment discipline and due diligence inputs like track records.

Confronted by these realities, most of the world's larger investors have chosen to stay on the sidelines. Their implicit choice is not to pick a way to play at all in this timeframe.

Meanwhile, as we saw in the ICO boom and bust, less sophisticated investors piled into the quickly generated whitepapers, buying tokens from people they did not even know. They applied Option 7 in the most unsophisticated way possible. In the next section we will discuss the best practices of early-stage investing, but suffice to say, none of them seemed to be applied in 2017 and 2018 by many of these ICO crowdfunding investors.

A handful of investors have been more thoughtful but still are becoming active in the blockchain space. Some have done so directly and actively forming their own venture-capital funds (Option 3), or have worked hard to become knowledgeable and valuable inner circle blockchain angel investors (Option 5). To do so, these new players are working hard to build out unique value-added capabilities that can help their portfolio companies succeed.

Max Mersch, general partner of Fabric Ventures in London, whose latest fund is focused on blockchain, says, "In the move from Web2 to Web3 the roles of founders and investors are all evolving. Founders need to lay the seeds for a project but also build a community of contributors, users, and maintainers of their networks. On the other hand, investors need to provide more than just capital—at Fabric Ventures we believe the best investors will actively participate within networks, stake their assets, and help build out the communities."

For our part, we created a blockchain fund of funds so that we could exercise the Option 4 strategy of becoming a passive investor in each of the best inner circle blockchain pure-play venture funds. We are very happy with our choice of our way to play—we are also direct, active value-added investors but only in a handful of blockchain startups (Option 5). We are pleased that we avoided the ICO boom and bust by not participating in sight-unseen token crowdfunding investing (Option 7).

Build an Investment Right to Win

Whatever option you choose for your way to play, it is important to then build a right to win by applying the best practices of investing under your chosen option and ensuring you can capture the KSFs for high investment returns.

We believe that the best practices of early-stage technology investing apply just as much to blockchain as they do to any other area of rapidly emerging new innovations. While it is too early for us to be able to prove that contention, we have yet to see any evidence that leads us to believe that it is any other way. Even though blockchain does raise the potential of new and distributed ways of operating, we don't see that this would dispel (one) the need for high-quality deal flow bringing in great teams and projects, (two) disciplined due diligence of those teams and projects, (three) good negotiation by the investor with regard to investment terms and conditions, and then (four) a great deal of value added to help the investment succeed. These four best practices have been researched extensively by academics focused on understanding how superior returns are captured in early-stage technology investing. Sidebar 12 provides a summary of the research derived from one of our earlier books.

Sidebar 12: Early-Stage Investing Best Practices Research

If early-stage technology investors get attractive returns, how do they do so? By being disciplined and ensuring they behave consistently across their investing activities, investors appear to raise the probability of achieving an attractive return. In his work on angel investors, Professor Robert Wiltbank shows that returns appear to be correlated with:

- **Due Diligence Focus**—conducting significant hours of collaborative expert-based due diligence drives returns. Sixty-five percent of the exits with below-median due diligence reported less than 1x returns whereas when angels spent more than 40 hours doing due diligence, they experienced a 7.1x multiple.
- **Industry Expertise**—angels earned returns twice

as high for investments in ventures connected to their own industry expertise, and many of their best exits came in this way.

- **Interaction with Portfolio Companies**—angels who interacted with the venture a couple of times a month after making their investments experienced a 3.7x multiple in four years whereas investors who participated a couple of times a year experienced multiples of only 1.3x in 3.6 years.

Investors wishing to achieve the attractive returns of angel investing would be wise to join and be active in angel groups that share these three characteristics in their organizational cultures. These behaviors are in marked contrast to investors that may do little due diligence or external professional due diligence that may be led by investors who themselves do not have expertise in the industries of the portfolio companies, and/or that may focus on being passive after the investment is made rather than at the extreme of active investing.

Source: Le Merle, M., & Davis, A. (2017). *Build your fortune in the fifth era*. Cartwright Publishing.

Need for Diversification

The final leg of the stool for developing a competitive advantage in investing into blockchain protocol projects and companies is that of diversification. Early-stage investing is high risk in that many of the investments you make will fail. Furthermore, it is a hit-driven business. A few investments will return most of the capital and drive most of the returns. In this context, the winning strategy across all options is diversification.

Sidebar 13 details the logic and research that supports this finding drawn from the world of angel investing. In blockchain we expect that the findings will be the same once we have sufficient investment history to be able to see the data and conduct the analysis. Remember, blockchain is only 10 years old, and most investing in the space only ramped up three or four years ago.

However, if we are correct, then the final step in capturing an investment competitive advantage, once you have chosen a way to play and applied the best practices for that option, is to make sure you are broadly diversified.

Again our chosen strategy of building a blockchain fund of funds was intended to do just this. By investing into 10 blockchain pure-play venture-capital funds, each of which may make 30 or more investments, even allowing for collaboration between the firms, we would expect a combined portfolio of more than 150 blockchain companies backed by the leading investors in the space. Our early indicators are positive on this front. This is obviously a powerful strategy if the goal is to be broadly diversified in a rapidly emerging area of innovation in which the future winners are unknown and the rate of failure will be high—both hallmarks of blockchain's future we expect.

Sidebar 13: Need for Diversification

In 2015 we asked more than 250 angel investors, who are members of Keiretsu Forum in the US and Canada, questions to assess what they had learned from the academic research in terms of the likely returns and the number of investments they would need to make in order to have a high likelihood of capturing those returns. Here are our findings:

- **Realistic Expectations**—angels have realistic and perhaps slightly low expectations for the return they expect from investing in their angel group. While the academic research suggests returns as high as 27% IRR, the angels surveyed were split between a group of 113 investors (45%) expecting returns between 10 to 20% and 140 investors (55%) expecting returns above 20%.

- **Need for Diversification Understood**—angels understand the need for diversification. The angels surveyed were split between a group of 106 investors (42%) who thought 15 to 30 investments sufficient and 144 investors (57%) who believed more than 30 investments would be necessary. Three investors thought that a portfolio of less than 15 deals would achieve diversification. Almost all of the angels surveyed believed that diversification would be beneficial towards raising the probability of getting the angel return.

- **Almost No Angels Achieve Diversification**—conversely, while understanding what diversification implies, almost no angels surveyed had a large enough portfolio to have a statistically high likelihood of achieving the angel return. The vast majority of the angels reported that they had fewer than 15 angel deals in their personal portfolios (206 investors or 81%). A group of 43 angel investors, or 17%, has between 15 and 30 investments. And only four, or 2%, had more than 30 deals in their personal portfolios of angel-backed companies.

Comparing these findings, it is striking to see that while 99% of angels believe that they need portfolios of more than 15 investments, only 19% of angel investors accomplished this level of diversification.

Given these findings, we then asked the angels the open-ended question, "Why are you undiversified, given that you understand the attractiveness of the expected angel return and the number of deals required to have a high likelihood of achieving it?"

The most common reasons given were along the following lines:

- *My net worth will not allow me to invest in enough deals. Since most companies have a $50,000 or $25,000 minimum investment size for a direct angel investment, I would need to dedicate too much into angel deals to build the portfolio size needed for diversification. I have a maximum of 10% of my net worth available for these types of investments.*
- *I believe in the thesis that I need to do many hours of due diligence and many hours of active participation*

in each deal. I can't support a large number of companies as an active angel investor—five to ten is about all I can cope with given the personal time commitments.

- *Even being active in Keiretsu Forum, I don't attend enough meetings to see enough deals that I would like to invest in, and certainly not seven to ten per year. I have a fulltime job, and with vacations and other commitments I may be attending six or seven times a year and investing two or three times a year.*

- *I am uncomfortable investing outside my own area of expertise even though I know other members in the room do have that deep industry knowledge. And within my own area of expertise I don't see enough good deals a year.*

- *I am based in city X, and that is where I see most of my deals. I don't see that many here each year that I want to invest in. If someone would show me deals in other cities that met my criteria and also which I could trust had been the subject of the discipline I expect when investing, then perhaps that would be a solution.*

In short, the angel investors surveyed for the most part had realistic expectations regarding the angel return, understood the need for diversification given the skewed nature of returns, and had a reasonable sense of what diversification implied in terms of portfolio count. But, because of practical considerations, they were unable to get there in terms of making enough investments in their own portfolios.

This provides clarity to perhaps the most important challenge facing early-stage technology investors. Given their capital constraints, their need to diversify, and their desire to benefit from the expected returns, they need to make many more small investments in early-stage technology companies. Source: Le Merle, M., & Le Merle, L. (2015). *Capturing the expected returns of angel investors in groups—Less in more, diversify.* Fifth Era LLC.

To summarize this chapter, the ways to create competitive advantage as an investor in blockchain include carefully picking a way to play from the options outlined and making sure the best practices that lead to superior returns are applied. In this way investors can hope for a successful approach to investing in blockchain. Diversification must, however, always be top of mind given the likely risk profile of any emerging area of technology.

In the next chapter, we review the same thought process as it applies to established companies that may want to position for competitive advantage in this new area of innovation, assuming that at sometime in the future it becomes important in their own industry and area of focus.

Chapter 15
Corporate Advantage

You have to be constantly reinventing yourself and investing in the future.

—Reid Hoffman

For corporate strategists who have gotten this far, we come back to the core question of how to develop competitive advantage in blockchain. Once again we will recommend the simple approach to strategy outlined earlier in this book:

- Begin with a vision of the future and the big issues that need to be solved in that future.
- Understand the enabling innovations and technologies that may be leveraged.
- Develop your strategy—make sure you have a way to play, you understand the key success factors (KSFs), and you can quickly secure a right to win.

Before we dive into this framework, just a few thoughts on corporate innovation more generally. In the last chapter, we described a number of learnings from the dot-com boom and bust. Being thoughtful about lessons from the past is just as important for established companies wishing to benefit from the rollout of a new and transformational internet protocol as it is for the investors—the subject of the previous chapter. First among those lessons was that some established companies were prepared to lean into innovation—both developing good innovation capabilities in-house and partnering well with external innovation networks. Others were not.

It has become clear over the last two decades that competitive advantage in innovation— and the huge economic rewards that come with it—accrue to the best of the disruptors and the handful of established companies that think and act like innovators.

The journey to become a successful innovator often requires a significant corporate transformation for large established companies—especially those that grew up in the Industrial Era. And without the right foundation, isolated innovation attempts can be a waste of time and resources, with seeds of good ideas or projects falling on infertile land and withering. Building an innovation capability at an established company is a major undertaking and can take many years—even with the committed leadership.

We have written extensively in our book *Corporate innovation in the fifth era* about a model of corporate innovation that is common across the most innovative companies, including Alphabet, Amazon, Apple, Facebook, and Microsoft, which we examined empirically, and many other successful established innovative companies. We won't repeat all of that thinking here, but we summarize the essential elements of the model below.

Fifth Era Corporate Innovation Approach

The lessons of the most innovative companies can be summarized in four elements. The most innovative large companies consistently do all four of them with commitment and intensity. Often the focus and intensity comes from a shared view of the burning platform—a clear-eyed shared understanding by the CEO, the board, and the leadership team that the company will not survive in 10, 20, 30 years if it is not successful at innovation. So innovation becomes a non-negotiable capability that needs to be honed and built, and receives serious investment, attention, and oversight at the board-level.

The four elements of the successful corporate innovation model are:

- **Drive Innovation Top-Down**—at the most innovative companies, innovation is a priority focus at the very top of the company—driven by the CEO and executive team and with proactive engagement and input from the board of directors. Innovation is driven top-down—as leaders live it in their own actions and behaviors, and require it of their team. Innovation is not considered a function. The chief innovation officer is effectively the CEO. Satya Nadella has bought this focus to Microsoft, Ross McEwan to RBS, Elon Musk at Tesla, Jeff Bezos at Amazon, and so on.

- **Embed Innovation into Strategies and Plans**—the second element is the extent to which the innovation strategy is developed and embedded into plans and actions across all corporate businesses and functions. Innovation is not just a set of activities and thinking that takes place in a central "innovation" function—often reporting to the CTO or a corporate development team looking to a few startups. The innovation strategy must start with a board-level shared view of the burning platform that frames the importance of successful innovation to the company's future. It incorporates a longer time horizon—often looking 10 or more years out. Traditional one- to three-year budgeting and planning cycles, and short-term financial metrics and tools can be major barriers to a successful innovation strategy. A good innovation strategy often takes a portfolio approach—understanding the importance of placing multiple bets across business units and outside them—the majority of which may fail—and being willing to dynamically shift course as things evolve in order to slowly build innovation muscle and see results. The innovation strategy then needs to be hard-wired into short-term and medium-term tactical plans with disciplined initiatives, funding, and metrics.

- **Build an Innovation Culture**—the third element is the creation of a culture that supports innovation and in which every employee—from the leadership, to functions, to frontline staff—is passionate about and engaged in finding superior and innovative ways to serve customers better than their competitors do. This ensures a high degree of alignment between the culture of the company and the innovation strategy. Innovation talent acquisition is a big challenge for many companies—how to build a culture and employee value proposition that allows you to attract and retain the key talent to drive successful innovation.

This goes beyond acquiring technology skills—e.g., data analytics, software, agile development—and applies more broadly to talent in human resources, marketing, finance, and operations. In many industries—a significant scarce resource is digitally savvy, innovation-leaning CEOs and business and functional heads—those who can lead the company into an uncertain future where new leadership skills, knowledge of new technologies, and experience in innovation are required.

- **Exploit External Innovation**—the final element is the importance of an external (versus internal) focus of innovation activities. The most innovative companies are tapping into the world's innovators and their innovations—rather than relying on breakthroughs created within the four walls of their own corporations. This requires an orientation and capability of working with external resources and ideas. This does not come naturally to many companies. In Sidebar 14 we detail the "external innovation toolbox" described in our book *Corporate innovation in the fifth era*. The external innovation toolkit includes 17 specific tools companies can use to work with the external innovation ecosystems. The tools help companies stay close to and take advantage of the most important breakthroughs that are relevant to their business.

Sidebar 14: External Innovation Toolkit

The external innovation toolkit covers 17 tools as follows:

Five external innovation tools focus on the academic community, researchers, and key opinion leaders:
- Grants and Scholarships
- Innovator Networks
- Key Opinion Leader Networks
- External Advisory Boards
- Joint/Collaborative Research and Development Agreements

Three further external innovation tools are focused on the developer community and technology entrepreneurs with companies in their very first stages of formation:
- Developer Certification and Support Programs
- Third-Party Incubators and Accelerators
- Corporate Incubators and Accelerators

Four external innovation tools are investment-oriented, enabling companies to become direct and indirect investors in early-stage ventures as well as providing access to promising new innovations as they gain traction:
- Crowdfunding Investments
- Angel Co-Investment Fund LP Positions
- Venture-Capital LP Positions
- Corporate Venture Programs

Five external innovation tools are focused on providing access to promising companies and their innovations by enabling licensing agreements, go-to-market partnerships, joint ventures, and acquisitions:

- Venture Exchanges
- In-Licensing Programs
- Go-to-Market Partnerships
- Joint Venture Programs
- Acquisition Programs

Source: Le Merle, M., & Davis, A. (2017). *Corporate innovation in the fifth era.* Cartwright Publishing.

With this as background, and assuming the company is committed to the importance of innovation in securing a sustainable future, we now turn to the more specific question of how to build corporate competitive advantage in blockchain.

The first step is to develop one or more robust views of the future.

Begin with a Vision of the Future

In the 1990s and 2000s a great deal of money was lost by those corporations that dove in first without a clearly defined understanding of what this all meant for their core businesses. At the same time, more often than not the companies with the bold visions were the new disruptors rather than the established players because they had a clearer vision of the future and were less encumbered with solving the nearer-term issues of the legacy business.

This implies a first challenge for established companies. Do you want to define a future vision and then move to shape it? Or will you instead watch as the disruptors define what is possible from the new and emerging technologies, all the while preparing yourself at the right moment to sweep in and acquire a more scaled version of the bold vision built out by someone else and then incorporate it into your own strategy?

Being at the very leading edge can mean that the first-mover corporations are at the "bleeding edge." The issue of how quickly to move and how to balance risk of failure with likely return is a complex one for established companies to navigate. However, in the risk/return equation, a clear-eyed understanding by CEO, board, and the chief risk officer, of the ultimate risk to the company of doing nothing—often an existential risk in disrupted sectors—can far outweigh the smaller risks of failed innovation.

For established corporations in industries in the early stages of disruption—as described above—we believe having an external focus and intelligence is essential; having strong antennae into emerging technologies and on the periphery that help inform the leadership's future vision is critical. Ultimately this responsibility falls with the board of directors who are the stewards of the company's sustainable success into the future. The board is ultimately responsible and must hold the CEO accountable for forming a future vision and understanding its implications for the company. If the CEO can't deliver on this, the board needs to find a new CEO.

A robust future vision or visions is an important starting point for those companies diving into blockchain and its associated technologies. For example, how does the blockchain protocol have the potential to change the future—future payments, future supply chain management, future identity and trust—and what are the opportunities created from this? The challenge for established companies is to craft their own future vision relevant to their own opportunity set.

The next task is to identify the big issues to be solved in order to reach that future vision. This can be difficult for established companies because they are so fully engaged in solving today's issues and the issues that their legacy operations have created. One of the biggest barriers to success for large companies in disrupted markets is that they consistently overcommit resources to sunsetting end-of-life businesses, products, and processes, and under-commit resources and investment behind the future vision. For example, the issue for a large retailer today might be bringing down the cost of physical delivery to their store network and ensuring those items most in-demand are always in stock. However, how does that change in a world where perhaps there are no more stores? The big issues to solve shift completely.

We often see that established companies have difficulty with creating a future view. Sometimes they find it easier to establish a distinct "skunk works" or "incubator division" rather than try to have today's business teams focus on a bold vision of the future and add a new set of priorities to their existing legacy list. Whatever the approach, established businesses at some point have to pivot efforts to focusing on tomorrow's issues that will form the basis of new ways to play. Most businesses, but not the leading innovators, over-allocate resources to the legacy business and under-allocate to the future vision opportunities.

Understand the Enabling Innovations and Technologies

This step is essentially the same for established companies as for emerging disruptors. The leadership of the company—including the board—has to be tracking and understanding the progress and potential of the next wave of innovations and technologies that are or might be relevant to their industry.

During the first phase of the internet's evolution, it was critical to be around the new protocol—observing, learning, building relationships, and gaining access—so that when things became real, it was possible to move fast. This meant having some degree of early activity. It also meant being very watchful of customers and new disruptive competitors:

- Watching how end users were adopting the new technologies, even in industries that might not seem directly relevant, gave great insights into the eventual course of adoption and change in your own industry. Those who did best during the rollout of the internet understood the types of value that could be delivered to their customers ahead of their competitors.

- Watching competitors very closely—including those that may seem to have been too early, flailing about, wasting money and resources—was critical. Because the glimmers of what would prove to be the "killer apps" in each industry were beginning to become apparent in those early competitor experiments.

- Getting close to the leading disruptor companies early also proved important. Much could be learned by seeing their early products and services, and gauging which elements of each were able to get traction.

We described earlier the importance of an external innovation focus and toolkit. Many companies at this time have in-house corporate development and corporate venturing teams, and central innovation groups and scouting teams. These groups can be very helpful for the company in understanding new and emerging technologies that might be relevant to the industry. These groups often spend a lot more time on the perimeter of innovation with mandates to scout, explore, test, and even invest in unproven but potentially important innovations relevant to the company's operations. Capital allocations, approved terms of engagement, and limits on how many bets and how large each can be are often well established. Many companies have clear rules of engagement that require active involvement of business units or product and service managers so that those working at the perimeter don't get overly carried away or too far from home as they roam outwards into the chaotic world of innovation.

Develop Your Strategy

Armed with a future vision of a blockchain-enabled world and the issues that need to be solved, as well as a deep understanding of new enabling blockchain technologies that can be leveraged, the next step is to develop your strategy—make sure you have a way to play, you understand the key success factors (KSFs), and you can quickly secure a right to win.

Make Sure You Have a Way to Play

In light of all of this input, the CEO and leadership team, along with the board of directors, need to define the corporate way to play. With new projects and startups this can be a clean-sheet-of-paper exercise. With established companies it often makes sense to lightly sketch some options and then move quickly to the KSFs before iterating back to refine the ways to play. The reason for this is that established companies by definition have existing capabilities, resources, and assets that may strongly tip the choice of which way to play they select.

Here we will reiterate that many corporate strategy development approaches can be overly complicated and not really fit for purpose in a period of rapid disruption. There is also a big cost to taking months and even years to develop and get agreement on detailed strategies when things are changing so quickly. There are many tools that can be helpful in developing a way to play for larger companies—as described earlier—scenario planning, wargaming, and so on. But the most important elements are a robust future view, engagement at the most senior levels of the company, and an agile approach that can change and adapt in real time based on new learnings, new external developments, and a willingness to experiment, make bets, learn fast, and iterate. Even for large companies, the best approach we have seen to developing a way to play is a well-facilitated, deep, and iterative working session with key leaders of the company—often including the board.

Understand the KSFs

In shaping the corporate strategy, the step of defining the KSFs against that new way to play is always a critical and valuable step. Once the short list of things that really matter has been defined, an established company is often in a good position to create competitive advantage since often one or more of the KSFs is already in their control. Here we have found that companies that are clear on the advantages they already possess are often very well positioned to create a powerful position for themselves within the emerging way of doing business.

There are many things that new disruptive innovation-based companies don't have that they need to get quickly in order to succeed—access to customers, insights from data, capital to fund investments, critical skill sets. Larger established companies often have exactly the things that startups need and can act as kingmakers. As a result, your company may be able to partner with emerging companies to succeed far more than either of you could independently. And if you can control that process, you may be able to create competitive advantage. A partial list of leverageable assets to consider would include:

- Insights into technologies, patents, existing solutions, etc. Data insights from existing customer
- In-house innovators who can help emerging company innovators do their work
- Existing products and services that can be the beneficiaries of new innovations

- Existing customers who can pilot and eventually roll out new innovations
- Sources of traction to cross-market to or use as early adopters
- Go-to-market capabilities in terms of channels, distributors, partners, and so on
- Service capabilities to support new innovations when they go live
- Regulatory licenses, capabilities, or relationships to get innovations approved and to navigate the issues associated with getting them successfully into new and existing markets
- International footprints to take innovations to other markets
- Capital to fund tests and pilots, and to provide runway to overcome initial failures

Of course there are many other leverageable assets that large corporations have. However, the key as noted earlier, is to know the most important KSFs that enable the chosen way to play rather than to catalog a long list of less relevant capabilities and assets.

Quickly Secure a Right to Win

In chapter 13 for entrepreneurs, we outlined several important elements to securing a right to win: build critical capabilities, lock up the best partners early, be ruthless in staying ahead of competition, and secure smart capital. For established companies many of these are just as important. However, we won't repeat them here.

In addition, there are other choices that become very important in moving from a way to play to a right to win. Since we are so early in the adoption curve of these new innovations, we cannot be sure what the complete list will eventually consist of. However, in the context of blockchain we see two critical choices surfacing around whether or not to drive industry collaboration, and whether to embrace open or private instances of the blockchain protocol. Each is discussed in turn.

Drive Industry Collaboration

The first phase of the internet's development demonstrated how difficult it can be to be successful alone, especially when complex cross-industry standards, regulations, processes, agreements, etc., need to be modified to enable the new technology to go live. Indeed, many of the best ideas from that period are surfacing again today as people explore whether this time the great promise of blockchain technology and digital monies and assets can improve the economic value of established industry business systems sufficiently that they will be prepared to change.

Often the only way to get traction is to develop industry consortiums. The companies that create and lead those consortiums and which do the early work are often best positioned to lead with the knowledge that they are able to capture early. So it is no surprise that we have begun to see the creation of industry associations and collaborative partnerships to work on initiatives across companies and industries. The IBM Hyperledger initiative, the Blockchain Collaborative Consortium, and the Global Blockchain Council are all examples of this phenomenon—just as we saw similar initiatives in the mid-1990s as large companies got to grips with the internet and its likely impact on them.

In their "State of Blockchains in 2019" report, Outlier demonstrates how companies are beginning to stand up infrastructure to allow other players to accelerate their own work. Examples from that report include:

- Hyperledger, the open-source blockchain initiative hosted by the Linux Foundation, added Alibaba Cloud, Citibank, and Deutsche Telekom, and 12 additional members in its fourth quarter.
- The Hyperledger blockchain was used to support the "Juncker Plan," an initiative by the European Commission to transfer €360 million to Spanish SMEs.
- The ability of R3 to raise $150 million to further develop its Corda blockchain from Singapore's Temasek demonstrated the willingness of more traditional investors to back enterprise offerings.
- Accenture deployed a custom procurement-to-pay solution for Thailand's Siam Bank on R3's Corda blockchain. The system tracks the sale of goods and collection of payments, and registers financing.

These partnerships are also important in the specific case of blockchain protocol because they allow for the creation of permissioned networks that do not allow open, public access.

Private vs. Public Debate

In the 1990s as the internet first gained traction we began to hear the private versus public network debate. At that time, the question was whether companies should have their own intranets, should partner to form "private walled gardens" within which multiple players might play in a secure space; or whether they should rely upon the public internet. In the first phase private intranets were widespread, and very few large companies opened up to the public internet. Then as time went by and the internet became ever more capable and the world's people began to move online, so the private intranets began to look less attractive. With narrower scopes, fewer users, and constantly falling behind from a core infrastructure perspective, private intranets became the exception rather than the rule for most customer-facing interactions. Today, private intranets may still be used for the work within the corporation, but they rarely are relied upon for the way to reach and sell to customers globally. In the latter regard, most companies have moved to the cloud.

The blockchain discussion is at that earlier stage today. Large companies are once again—appropriately—worried about the risks of moving their operations onto open, public blockchains. As a result, we are seeing most corporate prototypes being built on permissioned, private networks, which reduces the concerns about the hacking of data or the raiding of transaction history and activity. Furthermore, public, permissionless blockchains require the creation and maintenance of large independent communities without which they cannot survive. This creates a substantial challenge. Matthew Walsh, general partner at Castle Island Ventures, observed, "Investing in and building companies on permissionless blockchains require strict attention to the open-source communities that shepherd these protocols. Best-in-class companies and investors must understand not only the technical features and roadmap for the protocol—but also the culture and social fabric of these communities, lest they be caught deploying resources against a moving target."

Private networks are not without their own points of failure of course, and they also have some significant shortcomings when it comes to fully exploiting the potential of the blockchain protocol. However, for the immediate future we do expect most large companies and established industries to work on private networks as well as those controlled consortium "walled gardens" that are being established by leading technology companies.

Heed the Lessons of Lost Value

Before we leave this chapter, we would be remiss if we did not revisit the question of whether or not established companies need to move now or can afford to wait and watch.

This is a critical question for most large companies, and it is true that being at the "bleeding edge" of innovation is not always the best strategy. Conversely, we have seen many large corporations suffer badly through the strategy of ignoring innovations that at the outset seemed less relevant in their industry context. We recommend at a minimum a stance of active observation and preparation.

Sidebar 15 summarizes a study we conducted some years ago to assess the reasons for significant losses in economic value among public companies. The study showed that for the 103 biggest losers of economic value out of all public companies analyzed over the timeframe, over 80% of the time the reason for the significant value destruction was a strategic and/or innovation blunder; for example, being caught by surprise by a disruptive innovation launched by a competitor or new player; or showing a strategic inability to keep up with innovations in their own industry. This was in marked contrast to the much smaller count of biggest losers who had seen their economic value decline because of risks encountered in the other three categories analyzed: operational challenges; fraud/ethics/accounting/compliance issues; or external factors—such as political, economic, regulatory, or natural shocks.

The study emphasized to an even greater degree than we had expected that large corporate economic-value declines come from an inability of the company to create innovative strategies that ensure winning in highly competitive and dynamic industry settings.

In short, while the winners in economic value creation are the most innovative companies of the Fifth Era, the losers appear to be those that can't keep up with the new strategies of their industries and competitors: they are laggards in innovation in one way or another.

Sidebar 15: The Lessons of Lost Value

While many benchmarks of corporate practice start by looking at successful companies, a recent survey by authors Dann, Le Merle, and Pencavel took the opposite tack. They decided to study the biggest losers: companies that, in one way or another, had seen their fortunes go south over a 10-year period.

The researchers had gone through this exercise once before. In 2004, when the Enron, Tyco, and WorldCom scandals were fresh, they had surveyed thousands of public companies and determined that, contrary to prevailing wisdom, it was not compliance issues that were most responsible for destroying shareholder value. That distinction went to the mismanagement of strategic risks—those risks embedded in the top-level decisions made by the executive team, such as what products and services to offer, whether to outsource manufacturing, or what acquisitions to make.

The researchers' 2012 survey revealed the same culprit and suggested that it still leads to significant value destruction. Making matters worse, the sources of strategic risk have increased. Accelerating technology development is forcing the rapid adoption of new products, services, and business models; digital information is making organizations more vulnerable to theft and loss; supply chain disruptions quickly ripple around the globe, affecting both companies and customers; consumer connectivity via social networks can broadcast missteps instantaneously to millions of people worldwide; and natural, political, or regulatory shocks can reverberate widely. Companies must learn how to effectively anticipate and hedge against these and other risks in order to survive.

Studying the Biggest Losers

To more fully support this conclusion—that the lack of attention to risk destroys shareholder value— the researchers looked at the study in more detail.

- They analyzed US public companies with at least US $1 billion in enterprise value on January 1, 2002 (1,053 companies met these criteria).
- They calculated each company's change in enterprise value over the next 10 years and then indexed each company's annualized return to that of its industry benchmark to control for industry-specific effects.
- This allowed them to zero in on the biggest losers—the companies that experienced the most dramatic losses of enterprise value.
- Only 103 companies had annualized returns relative to their respective industry benchmarks that were worse than negative 10%. This group corresponded to the bottom 10% of performers in the overall sample.
- They checked to see if the companies on their list of the biggest losers were simply the weakest companies in one or two industries in terminal decline. But this was not the case. There was broad industry representation among the bottom performers.
- To get at the root cause of this lost value, they conducted an event analysis by going back to news reports, press articles, and brokerage reports for each of the 103 companies before and after their loss of value. Next they assigned each company's economic decline to one of four categories.

- The *first category* included major strategic blunders (such as new product or new market failures) or instances when a company was caught flat-footed by a major industry shift (such as digitization of content). They included failed mergers and acquisitions in this category, as well as dramatic shifts in major enterprise value drivers (for example, a major input cost) because these occurrences should have been foreseen. This category includes, for example, Time Warner and its widely criticized merger with AOL in 2000.

- In the *second category*, they grouped together major operational problems, such as supply chain disruptions, customer service breakdowns, and operational accidents, that had caused substantial shareholder value destruction. A high-profile example is the April 2010 Deepwater Horizon offshore oil rig explosion and leaks in the Gulf Coast, an event that wiped out more than US $50 billion in BP's shareholder value in the days and weeks following the accident.

- The *third category* included fraud, accounting problems, ethics violations, and other failures to comply with laws, standards, or ethics. During the 10-year timeframe analyzed, a few prominent examples were Tyco's accounting and discrimination lawsuits in 2002, and Tenet Healthcare's 2006 legal battles over improper medical and business practices.

- In the *fourth category*, they identified declines resulting from external shocks that were natural, political, or regulatory. They narrowed these situations down to circumstances in which the external event could not be controlled or easily anticipated by the company. For example, USEC, a supplier of enriched uranium for nuclear power plants, saw a sudden and sharp decline in enterprise value after the 2011 Japanese tsunami and ensuing nuclear disaster.

The results are unambiguous: among the 103 companies studied, strategic blunders were the primary culprit a remarkable 81% of the time. When the researchers segmented the data by industry and geography, they found some variations; for example, strategic failures are particularly acute in the financial-services industry, and Europe has more operational problems than the US or Asia. Nevertheless, strategic failure remained the major cause in these cases as well.

About half the time, the loss of value occurred gradually: over many months, or even years if the company took too long to grasp a changed strategic environment or lacked the agility to react. The other half of the time, the lost value occurred in a matter of months, weeks, or even days. Sometimes these sharp shocks were caused by strategic failure (for example, being caught by surprise when a competitor introduced a superior product). Sometimes they resulted from an operational issue, compliance problem, or external event that overwhelmed the company.

Source: Dann, C., Le Merle, M., & Pencavel, C. (2012). *The lesson of lost value.*

To summarize this chapter, competitive advantage for established companies rests upon a small number of complex challenges. These include the following requirements:

- Build a good innovation capability including a strong external innovation toolkit.
- Have a clear future vision or visions as relates to your existing business.
- Define the big issues that need to be solved.
- Identify how blockchain and a world of native digital monies and assets will apply to your business today and in the future—whether you develop it yourself or leverage the thinking of the disruptive innovators.
- Spend quality time with the leadership team and your board outlining bold visions for how you might play.
- Be clear on what are likely to be the KSFs, and determine which you already possess in order to iterate and select your initial way to play.
- Focus on quickly securing a right to win by building key capabilities, building connections with the best partners, and keeping a close eye on what competitors—new and old—are doing.

- Also in this early phase, driving industry collaboration initiatives can be a powerful way to create an option for a future right to win.
- These collaboration initiatives are likely to be private, permissioned prototypes at this point though in the longer term they may move to the open, public model.

It is clear from this chapter that it is still early days for blockchain, and the promise of the protocol for evolving the internet of today towards the internet of the future is still to be proven. However, we believe that every major established company needs to have a toe in the water right now. While it may be too early to jump right in—to be fully committed—in most industries, there are clearly some places where the race has already begun.

Those who don't begin to climb the curve of understanding are likely to miss what may be the greatest value-creation opportunity of our lifetimes—just as they did in the initial move to a connected digital world.

Chapter 16
Sovereign Advantage

The only way you get economic progress, real standards of living moving higher, is to have the savings of the society continuously invested in the cutting-edge technologies. And those technologies which are obsolescent get dropped out.

—Alan Greenspan

At the sovereign level, most governments are also beginning to embrace this new area of innovation. This is a large topic in its own right, and we will only touch upon it in this book although we have worked extensively on national industrial strategy, regional economic development, and clusters of innovation in the US including in California, for the ASEAN nations including China, and in parts of Europe. What follows are a few key points that we think are worth highlighting as nations seek competitive advantage.

Early Movers Getting to Work

Some governments like those of the more forward-leaning British Overseas Territories of Cayman and Gibraltar, and smaller countries like Estonia, Lithuania, Malta, Singapore, and Switzerland have moved quickly to create positive regulatory and legal climates to support the pioneers in blockchain technology. Others, including China, Korea, Japan, the UK, and the US, are at the very front of the technology wave with large commitments of time and capital to understand how to make the most of the technology for sovereign purposes. From a governmental perspective some of the principal areas investigation include:

- **Digital Monies**—should sovereign governments create blockchain-based digital currencies proactively rather than allow the formation of non-governmental monies?
- **Global Currencies**—will blockchain allow for a new reserve currency and store of value? And if so, should an independent project like bitcoin be allowed to capture that prize, or should a digital Dollar or Yuan or Euro contend for this position?
- **Security**—how can blockchain be used to create greater cybersecurity especially as warfare begins to become digitally driven?
- **Identity**—should governments migrate to citizen identities linked to blockchain registries? And how can other digital data be appended to these identities? China, Estonia, and India are leading with their initiatives in this space.
- **National Information**—what national information should be made public by attaching it to blockchain-based registries and indexes, and for what purposes?
- And so on.

The first successful applications of the blockchain protocol in government have now launched, and administrations around the world are watching as China begins to use its Social Index, Estonia moves to e-governance, and India establishes its first blockchain district. These being only a few of the more prominent examples taking place worldwide.

Clusters of Innovation Theory Applies

As the early adopters get to work at the sovereign level, they are beginning to ask about approaches that will lead to competitive advantage for their regions or countries. For us, this is not a new question to ask, nor is it one that will require new approaches or theory.

At its core, blockchain is primarily software, and even its more novel applications have seen proxies in the internet-related offerings that have already been successfully launched and adopted. We have well-established bodies of theory as regards how to ensure leadership and regional economic development in innovation clusters focused on software development and deployment. Without rehashing this subject here, we can summarize as follows:

- Clusters of innovation (COI) theory also applies to winning in blockchain at the regional level.
- This means understanding that the key players all need to be supported and motivated:
  - Blockchain entrepreneurs
  - The investors that back them, especially in their earliest phases
  - The larger companies that are needed to support deployment and adoption, especially if existing

products and services are being ported over to a new technological foundation

- Supporting players, such as lawyers, IP experts, accountants, marketers, and so on, who understand the details of successful operation in the new technology, are also critical to the successful creation of an innovation cluster.

- Governments must make sure of a supportive setting, including clearing away barriers to deployment, ensuring the legacy regulations and policies do not choke the growth of a new innovation, and conversely, at the appropriate time, establishing new fit-for-purpose regulations and policies.

- Successful clusters of blockchain innovation will be those that ensure they have a critical mass of all of the various constituents and that there is balance between the parts. There is no point in having large numbers of blockchain entrepreneurs if you don't allow them to access capital. Nor are you likely to succeed if you have large pools of investment capital, but you scare away all the entrepreneurs by putting in place policies that make it hard for them to get to work.

A lot has been written on clusters of innovation theory, so we will end here and allow readers to explore this topic in greater depth if they wish by accessing those works.

Who Governments Should Listen To

Governments should also watch carefully to ensure that established players with vested interests do not stifle new innovation before it is fully baked because their historical interests may be threatened by a new way of doing things. Their louder and more influential voice can drown out important ideas from an emerging but disorganized community of innovators and entrepreneurs.

In general when we visit countries and regional governments and we ask them who they have participating in their innovation hearings and public-private dialogues, we always find the following:

- Government officials from a breadth of areas are present
- Large companies have fulltime professional government affairs people at the table
- Academic experts including those drawn from state-owned research institutions
- Organized lobbyists including those who say they represent the "voice of the consumer" or "voice of the environment," for example
- Conversely, very rarely are the voices of entrepreneurs and early-stage investors heard despite the fact that they are:
  - Drivers of the innovations that are taking place
  - Few in number and very able to relocate any-where they want to go
  - In great demand from other locations who will attract and steal them away at the first chance

A practical early step for any region with the aspiration of becoming a global hub for innovation in blockchain is to make sure local entrepreneurs and early investors are at the table for any discussion regarding national or regional plans. Excluding entrepreneurs and early investors misses the whole essence of how innovation is taking place locally – it quickly becomes a battle to attract and retain talented entrepreneurs and to ensure there is enough private capital available to back their start up projects. Governments that understand this and are able to attract, retain, and motivate these people and the right behaviors will be able to gain a substantial competitive advantage over those that don't.

Location Does Matter

We were born in England. After more than 30 years in the US, we are now proud dual citizens. Britain has been an expert for centuries at making British Overseas Territories good places to get regulatory and tax advantages such that some companies, investments, funds, and so on, have chosen to locate their legal entities in those locations. Bermuda, Cayman Islands, Gibraltar, Jersey, Isle of Man—the list is long.

However, this does not mean those places are good bases for entrepreneurial entities and their people. Innovation occurs in innovation hubs. Finance and commerce occur in global economic centers. While users, communities, and partners are everywhere, there tend to be more in the more populated and more affluent parts of the world.

While regulatory and tax havens may have a part to play, governments that wish to position themselves well in the future world of blockchain-based innovation should make sure they are attractive for the fullest manifestation of a global digital hub and that entrepreneurs basing themselves there can easily serve global markets. This means establishing local regulations and policies that allow home-grown projects and companies to scale globally across jurisdictions. If you hamstring your local startups with local constraints that make it impossible for them to be global at birth, then they will simply relocate to other places where those constraints do not exist.

In the short final chapter of this book, we provide some closing thoughts.

Chapter 17
Final Thoughts

Victorious warriors win first and then go to war, while defeated warriors go to war first and then seek to win.

—*Sun Tzu*

Good strategy is not set by focusing on a one-year outlook and a set of one-year predictions. Indeed, the risk of missing the forest for the trees is always an ever-present threat when busy people focus on what they need to worry about this week.

The only way to win in the long term is to lift your head up from time to time and take the long view. Then informed by this long view, create your platform for competitive advantage before the war has even begun. As the Sun Tzu chapter epigraph written in 500 BC in *The Art of War* makes clear, this is not a new strategic approach. In blockchain a few of the leaders have begun to do just this, and they are preparing now for a much more competitive game, which is coming fast.

Whether you are a blockchain entrepreneur, investor, or established company, the thought process is always the same. Only its application and details vary. The process is:

- Establish a vision of the future and the big issues that need to be solved.

- Describe the enabling innovations and technologies that may be leveraged.
- Develop your strategy—making sure you have a way to play, understanding the key success factors, and quickly securing a right to win.

Then execute rapidly and with discipline, and be prepared to pivot so that you are ready even before others realize they are entering into a world of conflict.

We hope this book has been helpful and thought provoking and leaves you with a rationale for why blockchain matters, a sense of how you can best participate and benefit, and pointers for how you can win in the battle for blockchain competitive advantage that is now beginning.

We wish you the best in your endeavors. Please reach out to us with feedback or input or if you would like to continue the discussion.

References

Andrews, E. (2017). Is tech disruption good for the economy? Retrieved from https://www.gsb.stanford.edu/insights/tech-disruption-good-economy.

Angel Resource Institute at Willamette University. (2015). Halo report—2015 annual report. Retrieved from https://angelresourceinstitute.org/reports/halo-report-full-version-ye-2015.pdf.

Atkinson, R. D., Ezell, S. J., Andes, S. M., Castro, D. D., & Bennett, R. (2010). The internet economy 25 years after .com: Transforming commerce and life. The Information Technology and Innovative Foundation. Retrieved from http://www.itif.org/files/2010-25-years.pdf.

Central Intelligence Agency. (2018). The world factbook. Retrieved from https://www.cia.gov/library/publications/the-world-factbook/geos/xx.html.

Cumming, D., & John, S. (2014). The economic impact of entrepreneurship: Comparing international datasets. *Corporate Governance: An International Review, 22,* 162–178.

Dann, C., Le Merle, M., & Pencavel, C. (2012). The lesson of lost value. *strategy + business.* Retrieved from https://www.strategy-business.com/article/00146?gko=f2c51.

DeGennaro, R., & Dwyer, G. (2010). Expected returns to stock investments by angel investors in groups. Retrieved from https://www.frbatlanta.org/research/publications/wp/2010/14.aspx.

Deloitte (2018). Five basic areas of development for blockchain technology. Deloitte white paper.

De Treville, S., Petty, J., & Wager, S. (2014). Economies of extremes: Lessons from venture-capital decision making. *Journal of Operations Management, 32*(6). doi: 10.1016/j.jom.2014.07.002.

Cambridge Associates (2019). Cryptoassets.

DigiEconomist (2019). Bitcoin energy consumption. https://digiconomist.net/bitcoin-energy-consumption.

Dow Jones VentureSource (2018). Venture capital report. Dow Jones.

Faria, A., Barbosa, N. (2014). Does venture capital really foster innovation? *Economics Letters, 122* (2), 129–131.

Fidelity (2018). Annual Survey of Institutional Investors.

Friedrich, R., Peterson, M., Koster, A., Grone, F. & Le Merle, M. (2011). Measuring industry digitization—Leaders and laggards in the digital economy. Booz & Company. Retrieved from http://www.strategyand.pwc.com/reports/measuring-industry-digitization-leaders-laggards.

Grilli, L., & Murtinu, S. (2014). Government, venture capital and the growth of European high-tech entrepreneurial firms. *Research Policy, 43*(9), 1523–1543.

Ibrahim, D. (2010). Financing the next Silicon Valley. *Washington University Law Review, 87*(4), 717–762.

Jaruzelski, B., Le Merle, M., & Randolph, S. (2012). The culture of innovation: What makes San Francisco Bay Area companies different? San Francisco, CA: Bay Area Council Economic Institute. Retrieved from http://www.bayareaeconomy.org/files/pdf/CultureOfInnovationFullWeb.pdf.

Kelly, E. (2006). *Powerful times: Rising to the challenge of our uncertain world.* Upper Saddle River, NJ: Wharton School Publishing.

Kramer, R. (2009). Rethinking trust. *Harvard Business Review.*

Kunstner, T., Le Merle, M., Gmelin, H., & Dietsche, C. (2013). The digital future of creative Europe—The economic impact of digitization and the internet on the creative sector in Europe. Booz & Company. Retrieved from http://cercles.diba.cat/documents-digitals/pdf/E130122.pdf.

Laudicina, P., & Ambani, M. (2012). *Beating the global odds: Successful decision-making in a confused and troubled world.* Hoboken, NJ: John Wiley & Sons, Inc.

Le Merle, M., & Campbell, J. (2009). Building an external innovation capability. Booz and Company. Retrieved from http://www.fifthera.com/perspectives-blog/2014/12/9/building-an-external-innovation-capability?rq=Building%20an%20external%20innovation%20capability.

Le Merle, M., & Davis, A. (2016). *Build your fortune in the fifth era.* Cartwright Publishing.

Le Merle, M., & Davis, A. (2016). *Corporate innovation in the fifth era.* Cartwright Publishing.

Le Merle, M., Davis, A., & Le Merle, F. (2016). The Impact of internet regulation on investment. Fifth Era LLC. Retrieved from https://ennovate.withgoogle.com/uploaded-files/AMIfv94d-QN3_ypoQO23PVxaIcGtjEpAvj6PLGpSCDdGB6V27k8lb-ubT-MAHHrX_EClE3U4RRj9Zq73DkYhn8ZIU_Iahm8IQH_aID-FHvh5mZq8KyteCBe2IyVocz1o8iCy8FTGAKF_NCitY8dyP-4JyNMnXNIU7OcU1vxtJ4pEpJZYWS00nvNAYEs.

Le Merle, M., & Le Merle, L. (2015). Capturing the expected returns of angel investors in groups—Less in more, diversify. Fifth Era LLC. Retrieved from https://static1.squarespace.com/static/5481bc79e4b01c4bf3ceed80/t/56a1c90fdc5cb4477ee-852b9/1453443345617/2016+Fifth+Era+-+Less+in+more%2C+-Diversify.pdf.

Le Merle, M., & Le Merle, Max. (2016). Do VCs back start-ups? Ensuring start-ups are backed in an innovation cluster. Fifth Era LLC. Retrieved from https://static1.squarespace.com/static/5481b-c79e4b01c4bf3ceed80/t/56d29bf2f699bb6f0be6689c/14566430600 69/2016+Fifth+Era+-+Do+VC%27s+back+start-ups%3F.pdf.

Le Merle, M., Le Merle, T., & Engstrom, E. (2014). The impact of internet regulation on early stage investment. Fifth Era LLC. Retrieved from https://static1.squarespace.com/static/5481bc79e-4b01c4bf3ceed80/t/5487f0d2e4b08e455df8388d/1418195154376/

Fifth+Era+report+lr.pdf.

Mainardi, C., & Kleiner, A. (2010) The right to win. Strategy and Business Magazine. Retrieved from https://www.strategy-business.com/article/10407?gko=19c25.

Mason, C. M., & Harrison, R. T. (2002). Is it worth it? The rates of returns from informal venture capital investments. *Journal of Business Venturing, 17*(3), 211–236.

Mason, C. M., & Harrison, R. T. (2011). Annual report on the business angel market in the United Kingdom: 2009/10. Retrieved from https://www.gov.uk/government/uploads/system/uploads/attachment_data/file/32218/11-p116-annual-report-business-angel-market-uk-2009-10.pdf.

Outlier Ventures (2019). Corporate tracker. https://outlierventures.io/corporate-tracker/.

Nakamoto, S. (2008). Bitcoin: A peer-to-peer electronic cash system.

National Venture Capital Association (2018). NVCA 2018 yearbook. Arlington, VA: NVCA.

Porter, M. (1985). *Competitive advantage.* New York, NY: The Free Press.

Porter, M. (1990). *The competitive advantage of nations.* New York, NY: The Free Press.

Porter, M. (1998). *Competitive strategy.* 16th Edition. New York, NY: The Free Press.

Roach, G. (2010). Is angel investing worth the effort? A study of Keiretsu Forum. *Venture Capital, 12*(2), 153–166. doi: http://dx.doi.org/10.1080/13691061003643276.

SBA US Small Business Administration (n.d.). Small business facts and infographics. Retrieved from https://www.sba.gov/content/small-business-facts-and-infographics.

Schwartz, P. (1991). *The art of the long view: Planning for the future in an uncertain world.* New York, NY: Doubleday.

Schwartz, P., Leyden, P., & Hyatt, J. (2000). *The long boom: A vision for the coming age of prosperity.* New York, NY: Basic Books.

Smith, Adam. (1776). *The wealth of nations.*

Sohl, J. (2015). The angel investor market in 2015: A market correction in deal size. Center for Venture Research. Durham, NH: University of New Hampshire. Retrieved from https://paulcollege.unh.edu/sites/paulcollege.unh.edu/files/webform/Full%20Year%202015%20Analysis%20Report.pdf.

Srinivasan, S., Barchas, I., Gorenberg, M., & Simoudis, E. (2014). Venture capital: Fueling the innovation economy. *Computer, 47*(8), 40–47.

Statista (2018). internet usage worldwide—statistics and facts.

Tzu, Sun. *The art of war.*

Veretskaya, O. (2018) Behind the scenes of e-commerce: how online payments work.

Visa. How to run your business. Retrieved from https://usa.visa.com/run-your-business/small-business-tools/retail.html.

Wiltbank, R. (2009). *Siding with the angels. Business angel investing—Promising outcomes and effective strategies.* U.K.: British Business Angels Association.

Wiltbank, R., & Boeker, W. (2007). Returns to angel investors in groups. Angel Capital Education Foundation. Retrieved from https://www.angelcapitalassociation.org/data/Documents/Resources/AngelGroupResarch/1d%20-%20Resources%20-%20Research/ACEF%20Angel%20Performance%20Project%2004.28.09.pdf.

Acknowledgments

This book draws heavily upon everything we have learned from those early innovators and believers that shared their blockchain knowledge with us in the spirit of collaboration and evangelism that is a hallmark in this space. You are too many to mention by name. We are fortunate that you shared your wisdom with us before the mass media jumped on board. Thank you.

A special thank you goes to all the people at the blockchain projects that we are associated with. This list is long, and growing day by day, but at the time of writing it includes—1World Online, BitBull, Bitwise, Codex, Hadron, Linqto, Liquineq, London Block Exchange, ReadyUp, Securitize, Spark, and Veridium. You are the lead actors in this play, and without you this amazing breadth of innovations would just not happen. We are all here to help you, and we stand in awe of your passion and creativity.

We are just as excited to be limited partner investors—and in some cases advisors—at the leading pure-play blockchain venture firms including 1confirmation, 1kx, Blockchain Capital, Castle Island, CryptoOracle, Fabric, Future\Perfect, IDEO Co-Lab, and Pantera. We watch the excellence of your investment decisions and the commitment with which you support your portfolio companies, and hope you find the contents of this book helpful in your own endeavors.

We have been fortunate to enjoy the support of our own investors who have added their own capital to ours in the blockchain fund of funds that we are managing. Thank you for your trust and confidence. Thank you also, Bart Stephens, who not only has his fulltime role at Blockchain Capital but also finds the time to mentor and coach us as chairman of the advisory board of our fund of funds.

We wish to express our appreciation to Matthew's former partner at Monitor Group, and Alison's former professor at Harvard Business School, Michael Porter, who wrote the seminal books *Corporate Strategy* and *Competitive Advantage*. We don't for a moment wish to pretend that our writing can carry the theoretical and academic weight that Michael's contributions did. However, we purposefully chose to also focus on the search for competitive advantage—only in the world of ill-defined futures enabled by innovation rather than in established industries.

As to the writing of the book, Alison Davis and Matthew C. Le Merle authored this report, and all errors and omissions are theirs alone. Fifth Era Media was our publisher. Nancy Pile was our editor and Matthew McCarthy our proofreader. Robin Vuchnich designed the book's interior layout and the covers.

Finally, but by no means last, we thank our families and our readers. This book is dedicated to all of you. The blockchain protocol, or something even more powerful that takes it even a step further, will help us complete the journey towards a more powerful and more positive digital future—and the future is for our children and those yet to come. We offer this book to you in the hope that it will help you gain competitive advantage, whatever role you choose to take.

Thank you for reading it and getting to the last word.

Alison Davis
Matthew C. Le Merle
San Francisco, California, USA

About the Authors

Alison Davis

Alison Davis is co-founder of Fifth Era. She is an experienced corporate executive, public company board director, an active investor in growth companies and a bestselling author on the topics of technology and innovation. Currently she serves on the boards of Fiserv, Ooma, and RBS, and chairs the advisory board of Blockchain Capital. She was CFO at BGI (Blackrock), managing partner at Belvedere Capital, and a strategy consultant at McKinsey and A.T. Kearney. Alison has degrees from Cambridge (MA/BA) and Stanford (MBA). She was born in Sheffield, England, and has lived for the last 25 years in the San Francisco Bay Area where she raised her family with her husband, Matthew C. Le Merle. For more information, go to www.alisondavis.com.

Matthew C. Le Merle

Matthew Le Merle is co-founder and managing partner of Fifth Era and Keiretsu Capital—the most active early-stage venture investors backing almost 200 companies a year. Matthew grew up in England before living most of his life in Silicon Valley where he raised his five children with his wife, Alison Davis. Today he splits his time between the US and UK. By day he is an investor in technology companies and a bestselling author and speaker on innovation, investing, and the future. He has worked at McKinsey, A.T. Kearney, Monitor, Booz, and Gap. In his spare time, he enjoys reading, writing, and photography. He was educated at Christ Church, Oxford and Stanford, and is an adjunct professor at Singularity U. For more information, go to www.matthewlemerle.com.

Disclaimers

Income Disclaimer

This document contains recommendations for business strategies and other business advice that, regardless of our own results and experience, may not produce the same results (or any results) for you. We make absolutely no guarantee, expressed or implied, that by following the advice in this book you will make any money or improve current profits or returns, as there are many factors and variables that come into play regarding any given business or investment strategy.

Primarily, results will depend on the nature of your due diligence, product, or business model, the conditions of the marketplace, and situations and elements that are beyond your control.

As with any business endeavor, you assume all risk related to investment and money based on your own discretion and at your own potential expense.

Liability Disclaimer

By reading this document, you assume all risks associated with using the advice given herein, with a full understanding that you, solely, are responsible for anything that may occur as a result of putting this information into action in any way, regardless of your interpretation of the advice.

You further agree that neither we nor our companies can be held responsible in any way for the success or failure of your business or investments as a result of the information presented in this book. It is your responsibility to conduct your own due diligence regarding the safe and successful operation of your business or investment portfolio if you intend to apply any of our information in any way to your business or investment operations.

Terms of Use

You are given a non-transferable "personal use" license to this product. You cannot distribute it or share it with other individuals without the express written permission of the authors. Also, there are no resale rights or private label rights granted when purchasing this book. In other words, it's for your own personal use only.

Affiliate Relationships Disclosure

We make a number of references in this book to entrepreneurs, companies, or programs that we have invested in, worked with, or recommend. We have no paid affiliate relationship at all with any entrepreneur, company, or program we reference with respect to inclusion in this book.

Stay In Touch with the Authors

Visit

www.BlockchainCompetitiveAdvantage.com

to receive regular mailings and additional content about topics in this book, and to find out more about the authors.

CPSIA information can be obtained
at www.ICGtesting.com
Printed in the USA
BVHW031949090419
545087BV00001B/1/P

9 781950 248032